WOULD YOU LIKE TO SEE
YOUR BOOK ON THIS BESTSELLER LIST?

The Celestine Prophecy
Leaves of Grass
Tarzan of the Apes
The Tale of Peter Rabbit
Robert's Rules of Order
Huckleberry Finn
Lady Chatterley's Lover
Ulysses
Embraced by the Light
The First Whole Earth Catalog
The One-Minute Manager
What Color Is Your Parachute?

Believe it or not, all of the above books were originally published by their authors themselves. Today, in the age of the personal computer, the Internet, and World Wide Web sites, it is easier than ever to join them—with the information and resources provided by

The Complete Self-Publishing Handbook

David M. Brownstone and **Irene M. Franck** are a husband-wife team with extensive experience in publishing, packaging, and writing. Their many previous books, singly and jointly, include *The Dictionary of Publishing, Parent's Desk Reference (Parenting A-Z), Island of Hope, Island of Tears, The Silk Road: A History, Dictionary of the 20th Century, The Green Encyclopedia,* and *To the Ends of the Earth: The Great Travel and Trade Routes of Human History.*

THE
COMPLETE
SELF-PUBLISHING
HANDBOOK

NEW REVISED EDITION

David M. Brownstone
and Irene M. Franck

Previously published as *The Self-Publishing Handbook*

A PLUME BOOK

PLUME
Published by the Penguin Group
Penguin Putnam Inc., 375 Hudson Street, New York, New York 10014, U.S.A.
Penguin Books Ltd, 27 Wrights Lane, London W8 5TZ, England
Penguin Books Australia Ltd, Ringwood, Victoria, Australia
Penguin Books Canada Ltd, 10 Alcorn Avenue, Toronto, Ontario, Canada M4V 3B2
Penguin Books (N.Z.) Ltd, 182–190 Wairau Road, Auckland 10, New Zealand

Penguin Books Ltd, Registered Offices: Harmondsworth, Middlesex, England

First published by Plume, a member of Penguin Putnam Inc.

First Printing (New Revised Edition), July, 1999
First Printing, April, 1985
10 9 8 7 6 5 4 3 2 1

Ⓟ   REGISTERED TRADEMARK—MARCA REGISTRADA

LIBRARY OF CONGRESS CATALOGING-IN-PUBLICATION DATA:

Brownstone, David M.
    The complete self-publishing handbook / David M. Brownstone and
 Irene M. Franck.—New rev. ed.
        p.   cm.
    Rev. ed. of: The self-publishing handbook.   1985.
    Includes index.
    ISBN 0-452-28073-7
    1. Self-publishing—United States.   I. Franck, Irene M.
 II. Brownstone, David M. Self-publishing handbook.   III. Title.
 Z285.5.B75   1999
 070.5'93—dc21   98-50134
                                                         CIP

Printed in the United States of America
Set in Goudy and Serif Gothic
Designed by Eve L. Kirch

CONTENTS

....

PREFACE

A great deal has changed in publishing and self-publishing since the first edition of our *Complete Self-Publishing Handbook* appeared in 1985. Looking at that book, we realized that it was the last book we wrote on typewriters; since then we have authored another fifty books and more, all on our computers.

In the fourteen years since that first edition, most of us have come to use computers, the Internet has flourished, and new publishing economics have developed. Major technological changes have taken place in most aspects of manuscript preparation and production, as well as substantial distribution changes in the publishing industry.

In this period it has become far harder for most authors to find publishers for their work, and that is especially so for those who have not yet been published or who are as yet little published. At the same time, all the changes have made self-publishing a far easier and far less expensive alternative than ever before.

In publishing this second edition of our *Complete Self-Publishing Handbook*, then, our aim is precisely as it was fourteen years ago—to provide an entirely modern guide to the self-publishing process, in order to help authors who are seriously considering publishing their own works or have already decided to do so.

We have both been professionals in publishing, editing, marketing, and authoring for several decades. David entered the publishing trade in the late 1950s, Irene in the late 1960s. In the mid-1970s, after careers as publishers and editors, we both became authors, and since then have written some eighty works in approximately one hundred volumes. Aside from anything else, after all those years and works, it is rather a pleasure to do a book that can help other authors to "do their stuff."

Our thanks go to Penguin Reference Books director Hugh Rawson and the Penguin editors and production staff for so capably seeing this book through the production process.

Thanks also to our friends and colleagues in the publishing world, for their always valuable insights and for providing us with some of the estimates used in the practical cases in this book, especially Bob Pigeon, head of Combined Publishing, in Conshohocken, Pennsylvania; Joyce Jackson, Publishing Services Supervisor of Impressions Book and Journal Services (www.impressions.com), in Madison, Wisconsin; and Dale Adams, head of Editorial Services Online (www.edserv.com), in Washington, D.C.

Finally thanks, as always, to librarians throughout the northeastern library network, in particular to the staff of the Chappaqua Library—director Mark Hasskarl; the expert reference staff, including Martha Alcott, Maryann Eaton, Carolyn Jones, Jane Peyraud, Paula Peyraud, Carolyn Reznick, and Michele Snyder; and the circulation staff, headed by Marilyn Coleman—for fulfilling our wide-ranging research needs.

CHAPTER 1

Why Self-Publishing?

Self-publishing is an old and honorable pursuit. Walt Whitman's *Leaves of Grass*, Edgar Rice Burroughs' *Tarzan of the Apes*, Henry George's *Progress and Poverty*, Beatrix Potter's *The Tale of Peter Rabbit*, Mary Baker Eddy's *Science and Health*, *Robert's Rules of Order*, *Bartlett's Quotations*—all these and many other internationally famous books were originally published by their authors. Self-publishing is a well-worn path, rather than a new and untried publishing mode. For at least the last two centuries, authors have successfully explored most of the ways to move their books from desk to print to market. Indeed, the tradition goes back to the earliest days of printing, when writers like Erasmus mounted horses to carry their manuscripts halfway across Europe to printers, shepherding their work through each stage of publication.

Over a century ago, Ralph Waldo Emerson, Henry Wadsworth Longfellow, and Washington Irving were exploring several varieties of self-publishing. Emerson took his manuscripts all the way to finished books, paying a commission to his publisher for sales made; in his case, the publisher functioned much as some wholesalers do today. Emerson also spent most of his adult life on the lecture circuit and wrote a great many articles for the periodicals of his day—all of which helped sell his books. On the other hand, Longfellow went through the publishing process only as far as finished plates, and leased the plates to his publishers. Washington Irving went all the way through the publishing process, producing and selling several of his books as a self-publisher, including the *Sketch Book* and *The Knickerbocker History of New York*.

Some major authors have self-published all or most of their work. Walt Whitman, revered now, struggled for most of his life to put his work into print in self-published form. William Blake lived in poverty but managed to publish his own work. Samuel Clemens (as Mark Twain) self-published *Huckleberry Finn* and then the works of many other authors, turning into a publisher as well as writer and lecturer.

Some of those who were primarily self-publishers were extraordinary commercial successes. Mary Baker Eddy's self-published work provided the basis for the Christian Science movement, for example, and has sold millions of copies. Edgar Rice Burroughs published most of his own body of work, at great profit.

Many authors—all the way from Byron, Carl Sandburg, and T. S. Eliot to Zane Grey—have self-published their early work. Many others have published their own work and have had their work, once in print, picked up by commercial publishers and widely distributed. This is quite a strong modern trend, as well as a historic one, that was the pattern for such modern best-selling books as *The One Minute Manager, The First Whole Earth Catalog, What Color Is Your Parachute?*, and *The Celestine Prophecy*. It was also what happened to *Lady Chatterley's Lover, Ulysses, Robert's Rules of Order, The Tale of Peter Rabbit*, and *Progress and Poverty*. It happened to Tom Paine's *Common Sense*, too—only Paine had no adequate copyright protection in the eighteenth century, and his work was stolen by his printers.

It is clear that a great many authors have published their own work, often with considerable literary and commercial success. Indeed, it is all too tempting to stress those success stories, and thereby distort reality. For every Emerson, Whitman, and Sandburg, there are a hundred authors whose names we no longer remember. For every great commercial success—for every Zane Grey, Edgar Rice Burroughs, Bartlett, Robert, or Eddy—there are hundreds of hopeful authors who wrote and perhaps published a book or two, and then moved on. No matter; serious people write because they have something to say, whatever the financial rewards. Success stories are warming and sometimes enlightening, but you cannot expect to make your first million dollars out of your self-published book—or, for that matter, out of a work published by a big "New York publisher."

That said, it is clear that self-publishing has become a strong alternative to traditional publishing for many authors today, making it possible to profitably publish works that might otherwise never find a commercial publisher.

Self-publishing is not for everyone, nor is it equally suitable for all types of books. But there have been major changes in the relationships between authors and publishers, in the economics of publishing in general, and in the bookselling marketplace. At the same time, the advent of the computer, coupled with the development of much less expensive production technology, has greatly cut production costs. During the 1990s, increasing numbers of first-time and special-subject authors have been able to publish electronically, reaching their audiences on-screen, without ever going into the body of expenses associated with creating print-on-paper books.

The Situation of Authors Today

This is a time of considerable change in the linked worlds of writing, publishing, and bookselling, and the pace of change accelerates. We live and write in a world in which mass audiences turn toward television and formula fiction, and away from more demanding and more literate work. Casually written, poorly edited, badly produced pop psychology and how-to books crowd serious nonfiction off the bookstore shelves. Publishers, many of whom are in deep economic trouble, reach for the kinds of safe, potential bestsellers that will keep them afloat and perhaps even modestly profitable. Writers of good, serious work find it very difficult to secure publishers.

That is all true; it has also been the standard lament of writers, publishers, and booksellers for many years now. We can continue to wait for better times that may not come, or we can analyze our situation and see how to successfully publish and distribute our work in changed circumstances.

Several trends have a great deal to do with the situation of authors today. By far the most important of these is the continuing move from print to screen forms, which began with the advent of the movies, accelerated greatly with the introduction of television, and is now accelerating once again as special-purpose television and computer-connected screens of several kinds appear in homes and workplaces. It is likely that, in the long run, most of humanity will be reading print on screen and that books will thereby complete an historic transition from print to screen, with far larger numbers of very literate readers—and very prosperous writers—than ever before. But in this period, that mass move from print to screen means fewer readers for our books now as book-reading habits fade and screen-watching habits grow.

Another major trend is the fragmentation of general book markets into special-interest book markets. This has made it very difficult for many general trade publishers to reach for the natural prime audiences of many books through traditional bookstore sales outlets. Some publishers that reach for narrow book-buying audiences by mail, and are able to charge prices high enough to justify the intrinsically high cost of mail solicitation, have done rather well; this is notably true of some professional and reference publishers. Many publishers are trying to develop alternative outlets for their books, as by direct selling over the Internet. Most general trade publishers continue to rely mainly upon bookstores for hardcover and trade paperback book sales, however, at a time when massive chain store operations are driving large numbers of independent bookstores out of business. That has meant reaching more and more for lowest-common-denominator mass audiences, while competing for limited bookstore display space with many other publishers. Here Gresham's law has been proven as operative for books as it is for money: the bad books drive out the good.

This is a climate in which we can expect publishers, especially trade book publishers, to continue to be wary of committing considerable sums of investment money to new books from any but very "bankable" authors. Even some very well-known authors, including many celebrities, will have difficulty in placing some of their proposed books. Investment money will be forthcoming, certainly, as it is now for some books thought to be relatively "sure" to show a profit. However, we cannot expect much to be available for the publishing of good or nonstandard books, especially by unknown authors.

We should not expect commercial publishers to behave otherwise, by the way. A marketplace economy has its own imperatives; even those publishers who continue to care about publishing good books must spend most of their time acquiring books that will sell well and generate profit. This is clearly so for publishers that have become the subsidiaries of other companies; publishing executives who fail to reach profit goals are soon replaced, even if they have continued to make money for their companies. This is true for independent commercial publishers as well, though independents can—and in some instances do—try very hard to continue to publish good books. Yet independent publishers must also pay their bills, pay interest on borrowed money, keep stock values up, and pay dividends to often impatient investors. In the long run, the need for profit is the same for all commercial publishers, though some independents need not seek to profit as much and as consistently as do publicly held or conglomerate-owned publishers.

In one sense, the fragmentation of book markets has been a bad thing for many authors, in that it has become more difficult to place many kinds of books with commercial publishers. On the other hand, this trend brings with it opportunity. Much more on this later, but for now let us point out only that authors are not hindered by the same kinds of profit imperatives that commercial publishers face. Nor do authors have to pay for expensive office space or support substantial numbers of employees, some of them making a good deal more money than do most authors. An author will usually find it much harder to reach national markets with a general-audience book than will most commercial publishers. But a self-publisher will very often be able to reach local, regional, or narrow markets far less expensively and more profitably than a commercial publisher. All of this means that an author may very often profit decently and sometimes even handsomely from a book that a commercial publisher would not—and really should not—be willing to publish at all. Putting it a little differently, a book that may be quite properly seen as a foolish gamble by a commercial publisher may be a perfectly sensible candidate for publication by its own author.

Production Economies

To a considerable extent, self-publishing has become more attractive because of the development of a fourth major trend, which is in the economics of book composition and manufacturing. Self-publishing authors today face far more favorable composition and production costs than did authors in mid-century. The author who wanted to self-publish before the mid-1950s had to compose very expensively in hot-metal type and then go on to produce hardcover books with printers whose equipment and attitudes made short-run printing very expensive indeed. A page of ordinary and straightforward type might typically cost $12–$15 in hot metal, and much more if tabular setting were involved. A short run of hardcover books might easily cost $5–$10 per book. And that was in forty-five-years-ago dollars; $12–$15 per page in the mid-1950s translates into roughly $70–$90 per page in the late-1990s, and $5–$10 per book translates into $30–$60. Trade paperbacks were then just beginning to be published, and had little acceptance among book buyers and librarians.

Even thirty years ago—after the composition revolution that replaced hot-metal type and metal printing plates with cold type and photographic processes—composition costs were much higher than they are today. A publisher thirty years ago might have been pleased to buy a page of ordinary book type for $6–$10 and a short run of hardcover books for $2–$4 per book. That translates in real dollars today roughly into $30–$50 per page for composition and $10–$20 per short-run book.

Today, self-publishing authors can use their personal computers as extraordinarily inexpensive composition machines and may be able to produce composed pages for as little as $2 per page in today's dollars, even including something for their own time spent in typing corrections and coding the text into the desired format. In real dollars, that is about 2–3 percent of what that page would have cost to set forty-five years ago, and about 4–6 percent of the real-dollar cost thirty years ago. Authors composing with professional book production people may still pay $6–$10 per page today, but that is, in real dollars, only a small fraction of the composition costs in the late 1960s.

Today's hardcover book is, for long runs, no more expensive than it was thirty and fifteen years ago, and for short runs is somewhat less expensive in real dollars, given new technology and manufacturing approaches. But today's short-run trade paperback is strikingly less expensive than yesterday's hardcover book, and that is the main real comparison for self-publishers. Today, the relatively short-run, modestly sized trade paperback—which can be sold for almost as much as a hardcover book—may cost as little as a dollar to manufacture, as against $3–$8 for its hardcover equivalent.

Hardcover or soft, the economics of self-publishing have changed greatly, and much for the better. Small wonder, then, that self-publishing authors and small publishers are multiplying. The wonder, really, is that so few large trade publishers have found it possible to adapt their operations to the new and very favorable economics of small-scale publishing. Most large professional and reference publishers have long since done so.

Distribution Changes

We are also seeing major changes in book distribution techniques and patterns. Mail-order selling has become rather a big business in books, as throughout the economy. This has meant that both highly specific mailing lists and very skilled mailing houses have become readily available to self-publishing authors, as they have long been to large businesses. As a result, authors can sell their books by mail directly to narrow specialist markets far more easily and profitably than ever before.

Along similar lines, many self-publishing authors have found it possible to sell their books directly on the Internet. Some have even gone all the way to selling their books on the Internet in electronic form, without going to print-on-paper. However, many questions have yet to be solved before self-publishers can expect stable profit from purely electronic book fulfillment.

Direct face-to-face bookselling opportunities have also increased, as authors read and speak to college audiences, conventions, meetings, and television audiences. Authors who can link up speaking and teaching activities with self-publishing can often achieve excellent and highly profitable book sales, making far more money and gaining far more control than those who sell their books for a publisher on tour.

This period has also seen the rapid growth of the chain bookstore and, with it, the possibility of thousands of book sales from a single chain placement. That is both hazard and opportunity, however. Chains may "buy" big; they also may return large numbers of books, perhaps even 50–60 percent. That can turn what should have been a modest success into a bankrupting failure, for the self-publisher may have printed and paid for thousands of books that cannot be sold.

In addition, increasing numbers of independent book representatives today handle book sales for many publishers at a time. Some of these are very small publishers who are essentially author-publishers or groups of author-publishers.

All of the above developments can be highly favorable to self-publishing authors, if properly understood and worked with. We will have more, much more, on the opportunities stemming from new techniques and patterns of book distribution later on in this book.

During the 1980s and 1990s, we have also seen the emergence of a substantial body of skilled independent publishing professionals, many of them capable of taking a manuscript all the way from early developmental editing right on through production and sale of finished books. Given their presence and accessibility on the publishing scene, even the most timorous authors need no longer see self-publishing as anything but a viable alternative to commercial publishing.

Publishing Difficulties

Beyond these major trends, several developments within the publishing industry itself have had adverse impact upon writers. Together these have caused authors to consider the self-publishing alternative much more seriously than ever before.

Not so long ago, some of the best advice you could give a new writer was to find a good agent, preferably someone working in or very near the New York metropolitan area, who knew everybody in and everything about the very small and incestuous world of New York publishing. With that kind of agent, assuming the writer had basic writing and thinking competence, it would be only a matter of time before the writer's books began to be placed. That was quite true not so long ago, but not now. Today, even experienced and well-connected agents often find it hard to place the work of many established clients, much less the work of newcomers. Oh, some do, of course; there are still real success stories to tell. But in this period it is very hard to find a well-established agent who will seriously take on newcomers. Worse, even with an established agent, many authors, especially new ones, have difficulty placing books with a publisher.

If an author does place a book, that book is more likely than before to be published as a trade paperback—a paperback book marketed mainly through bookstores, but in size and content like the hardcover books around it. Except for the price. Trade paperbacks cost less than hardcover books, making them attractive to many book buyers.

The problem for the author of a trade paperback book is that royalty rates—and therefore the advances against royalties offered by publishers—are much smaller than for equivalent hardcover books. The standard hardcover royalty is 10 percent of the cover price for the first 5,000 copies sold, 12½ percent for the second 5,000 copies sold, and 15 percent thereafter. The standard trade paperback contract is 6 to 8 percent of the cover price for the first 10,000–20,000 copies sold and 8 to 10 percent of the cover price thereafter.

For example, a hardcover book selling a total of 10,000 copies at $20 each is likely to yield approximately $22,500 in royalties.

Royalty income for $20 hardcover book:	
5,000 copies @ 10 percent royalty	$10,000
5,000 copies @ 12½ percent royalty	12,500
Total royalties	$22,500

However, a trade paperback edition of precisely the same book selling 10,000 copies at $15 may yield as little as $9,000 and no more than $12,000. If you take the probable sale of the book down to 6,000 copies—a reasonable figure for many works of both fiction and non-fiction—the hardcover royalties become a very modest $12,500. But the trade paperback royalties become a very small $5,400. The royalty advance the publisher actually offers a writer will reflect the royalties expected to be earned by the book, for publishers want to do books that "earn out" their royalty advances. All of this makes the economics of writing books to be sold by trade paperback publishers rather grim for authors in this period.

Neither can book authors reasonably expect to "piece it out" through hard times with magazine articles, as might have been possible in the last generation. Magazine-writing markets are, if anything, in worse condition than book-writing markets, with article rates generally far lower in real dollars than at any time since the Great Depression.

Writers' unions can be helpful, especially when dealing with those publishers who see difficult times for writers as an opportunity to behave as abominably as they possibly can, without a shred of even ordinary business ethics. But writers' unions will not solve the deep and persistent problems besetting the general trade book industry, which publishes most of the kinds of books authors want to write.

The Self-Publishing Alternative

Given these problems, more and more authors are seriously considering the self-publishing alternative, along with the possibility of publishing through very small publishers owned by others or through authors' cooperatives. Our focus here will be on self-publishing, though much of the book will apply to the small publisher and cooperative alternatives, as well.

We speak here of *self-publishing*. Becoming the publisher of your own written work—whether in book, mixed media, or nonbook form—means taking ultimate responsibility for the whole process of preparing, producing, selling, physically distributing, and collecting money for your work, as well as for all the business functions which inevitably relate to the funding of any business, however small. Make no mistake about this: the decision to publish your own work is a decision to undertake everything any other publisher might undertake in behalf of your work, within the context of running a small—sometimes a very small—business of your own. No matter how skilled the help you secure, the financial and publishing responsibilities are ultimately yours. And however you measure profit or loss, in dollars and intangibles, they are yours, too.

You may self-publish work that you have written alone or with a co-author, or work that is only in small part yours, as when you do an anthology or a handbook composed mainly of articles written by others. Should you publish your own work and then move into the publication of works written by others as well, then you will become both self-publisher and publisher. Should you stop publishing your own work and continue to publish the work of others, you will become a publisher, whatever work you continue to write for publication by others. These are not merely matters of definition, for they identify focus—and hazard.

For writers, one of the key hazards connected with self-publishing is the possibility of becoming so fascinated with the process of publishing that they lose concentration upon writing. Publishing is fine if it is what you really want to do. However, most writers write because they must, and a frustrated writer turned almost-full-time publisher is likely to be half-satisfied—and probably not much good at—either writing or publishing.

For the dedicated writer, self-publishing is essentially a defensive set of moves, aimed at getting written work from desk to audience, and at making enough money to at least survive and be able to write on many other days. If a little commercial success as a publisher turns you away from your writing, then you have paid far too high a price for that little bit of success. But if, on the other hand, it allows you to keep on writing, then it is success indeed.

Self-Publishing Is Not Vanity Publishing

Let us distinguish here between taking the responsibility for publishing your own work, which is self-publishing, having your work published by a publishing house, which takes some risk in publishing that work, and paying a publisher to publish your work. Neophytes sometimes mistake this last alternative for self-publishing, but it is really an expensive blind alley: vanity publishing.

It is very easy to assume that, if you are willing to spend time and money writing and publishing your own book, it is essentially the same thing and perhaps much more efficient to just write the book and pay an experienced publisher to produce and market it. After all, many small publishers—and a startling number of large ones—pay little or nothing in the way of advances against royalties. The vanity publisher who so obligingly advertises for authors in a book review or writer's magazine wants only a few thousand dollars to do it all—and, of course, disarmingly supplies proof stories about how so many have made money by taking this very easy path to publication.

Well, it would make sense if vanity publishers actually produced all the books they imply they will produce; if they really actively sold books, instead of relying upon the payments of authors for their profits; and if most people in the book trade did not consider a vanity press imprint to be the kiss of death for a book. But if all those things were true, vanity presses would be reputable publishers rather than traps for unwary, hopeful, rather bemused authors.

A vanity press is a publisher that advertises for and otherwise seeks out authors, contracts to publish their books, and charges them some thousands of dollars for doing so. Vanity presses often produce a few books, holding the rest of the promised press run in sheets rather than in bound books. They advertise minimally, usually with group advertisements for many books in a few book reviews or other periodicals, and do not really expect to sell many copies of your book. They are quite happy when a book sells decently, almost always due to its author's promotional efforts, but will do nothing much to help it sell, as their essential business is to make profit from the author's payments to them. Their promised editing assistance usually turns out to be a very minimal copyediting job, with good, bad, and simply awful work all treated equally and made into books. Most vanity publishers successfully protect themselves against charges of actionable fraud with very carefully constructed disclaimers and author-publisher contracts. Note that vanity publishing is sometimes mislabeled subsidy publishing. That is quite different, being the publishing of works supported by institutional grants of several kinds.

For those few authors who want only to see their work in print, who care little or nothing about money, and who are unwilling to take even the most elementary steps toward self-publication, a vanity press publication may make sense. But such authors are few and far between. Most authors who turn to vanity presses do not know what they are getting into, and have no idea that there are entirely feasible and less expensive solutions, which are far more acceptable in the publishing marketplace.

Even aside from the cost, trying to sell a book with a vanity press imprint on it is like pushing a huge stone uphill. If you have any doubt at all about that, go into several reputable bookstores, with the names of some presses that advertise for authors, and look for those publishers' books on the store shelves. If you feel the need to go further, go to the public library and search for those publishers' books on the library's shelves. If you see one, turn to the first leaf of the book, and you are quite likely to see that it was donated to the library by its author or a member of the author's family. The truth is that bookstores seldom stock and libraries seldom buy vanity press books; they have a bad reputation among booksellers and librarians.

If you are a neophyte and have some money you are willing and able to spend on your book, almost any publishing mode is better than going to a vanity press. It is far better, for instance, to hire a competent freelance editor, who may cut your book up one side and down the other, but in the process may help you create a book you can really be proud of. Then you can learn something about self-publishing and publish it yourself, or find a small or large publisher that is willing to put some time and money into producing and selling your work. Either way you will still probably get little or no advance against royalties, and you will still invest some money in making the book fit for publication and then publishing and marketing it. But you will have written and published a real book, with your self-respect intact and with a real chance for recognition and even for some commercial success in the book marketplace. You would have no such chance with a vanity publisher.

For many authors, self-publishing is, from the start, at least as good a way to go as commercial publishing. For others, the choice can go either way, depending upon capital and skills. And for others—including many who have previously taken the standard commercial publishing approach for granted—self-publishing may provide control, flexibility, and the ability to make far more money than their work has so far yielded.

Successful self-publishing requires some learning, though. To self-publish, you must know something about the publishing process: how to handle the main specifics of editing, manuscript preparation, composition, manufacture, book costing, pricing, mailing, selling, promotion—and a little bit about how to start and run a small business, too. It sounds like a lot, doesn't it? Well, reflect on the fact that young people just a few years out of college—and with no previous training or experience in publishing, editing, or marketing—occupy many key jobs in American publishing and bookselling today. Then take another look at yourself and your capabilities. There is no reason at all for a writer to back away from self-publishing because of imagined lack of aptitude and training. With sufficient motivation and patient attention, any writer can learn how to publish his or her own work, and do it well. That makes an overview of the publishing process the next order of business, and the next chapter of this book.

CHAPTER 2

· ·

What You Need to Know About the Publishing Process

If you want to publish one book or a hundred books, your own book or the books of others, you must know a good deal about the several intertwined processes involved in bringing a book before its audiences, as well as something of the business side of publishing. No, you need not be able to run Random House or McGraw-Hill to self-publish your own work, but the essential publishing and business processes are quite the same, whether your book is self-published or brought out by a large commercial publisher. They differ only in such subsidiary matters as the sequencing of some events, in financing arrangements, and, usually, in scale. Here is an outline of the publishing process, function by major function, aimed at providing an overview of the entire process. (A flow chart showing the process is also provided in Appendix 2.) We will discuss each function and the choices surrounding it in more detail later on in this book.

Writing and Editing

First, you have to write the book. That is a big, basic difference between self-publishing and being published by a large commercial publisher. When you do a book with a commercial publisher, you may submit a proposal, with an outline and probably some sample material, get a contract and an advance against royalties, and settle down to write the book. While you are writing—and especially once your publisher has a good idea as to when you will really complete the book—your publisher will be developing promotion and marketing plans, and may be seriously engaged in attempting to sell book club, paperback, foreign, serialization, and other subsidiary rights many months before you even finish. But when you self-publish, you must write the book first, because until you have something very substantial to show—at least bound proofs of your completed manuscript—you are unlikely to be able to do any serious marketing, promotion, or selling of subsidiary rights. This difference in the sequencing of selling activities could add up to a significant set of disadvantages for self-publishers—except that only a few commercially published books get the full range of prepublication attention described above, and those are increasingly the "blockbusters" that commercial publishers seek from "bankable" authors.

So first the book itself needs to be written, from the original idea through the creation of your completed manuscript, and with as little diversion from the writing process as possible. Most of us need to concentrate completely while writing a book. To the many potentially jarring distractions outside our control, it is unwise to add a too-early concentration on publishing plans and mechanics. Remember that a book can take far longer to write than you had supposed. Contacts made too early may have to be reestablished and plans redone if you finish your book considerably later than you had planned. Freelancers can become unavailable, printers may move or change price schedules, and your own plans may change a great deal during the months or years in which you are creating a book. For self-publishing authors, then, the cardinal rule is "first write the book."

Only if you have published with others or have self-published previous books should you be deeply involved in the publishing process while writing, and then only as a matter of necessity. When writing a book, do your best to set aside as many large blocks of prime time as possible, minimizing other potentially distracting involvements during those periods. You may be able to turn out sound work while you are tired and distracted; if many writers couldn't do that, far fewer books would be written. But if you can do good work when you are not at your best, consider how much better your work can be if you are fresh and fully focused for long enough periods to allow you to get deep into your work.

To write the book before seriously starting to publish and sell it is not to ignore its marketplace possibilities. Whether by choice or simply in fact, you are likely to be writing for audiences that can be defined, and that definition supplies the context within which all publishing decisions will be made, including production and marketing decisions and expenditures.

Although this book is about publishing rather than writing, one publishing function—developmental editing—straddles both fields and is of great importance for the writer, especially for neophytes. A developmental editor—preferably an experienced editor other than the author—acts as a guide and sounding board, giving professional advice on the development of the work in its early stages. Securing competent developmental editing help early in the writing process can be vitally important, whether you are self-publishing or publishing through others. Indeed, this key element of publishing is fast disappearing from commercial houses and increasingly must be supplied by authors themselves.

Whether or not you work with a developmental editor early on, creating a piece of work—of any length, in any form—requires writing, rewriting, editing, and rewriting again, as necessary. If your book has illustrations, it may also require the creation of maps, drawings, charts, graphs, photographs, and other illustrative material. In the course of preparing your manuscript, you may work with such people as artists, mapmakers, and picture researchers, who may produce, research, or secure such illustrations. You may also need to secure permissions to quote or reproduce material from other copyrighted works, possibly using an experienced editor to help you.

Ultimately, on your own or with the help of various experienced people, you will have created and refined a final manuscript. At that point, having finally set the order and content of the materials in your book, you will be able to also create a final title page; a preface, foreword, and introduction, if any or all of these are desired; a table of contents; and any other desired items of front or back matter. Some nonfiction authors also then begin to go through their manuscripts to prepare word and subject lists for their indexes, but in our view that is premature. You will most efficiently prepare an index only when you have before you a final set of numbered page proofs, and that is still several steps away.

Then you will move into the copyediting of your finished manuscript. In a few rare and special situations, you may choose to do all editing functions yourself—that choice may be entirely valid if you are publishing poetry, for example. But in almost every other instance, editing your own work is an elementary and probably disastrous error; it is a job for a professional other than yourself. If you have worked with an editor to develop the manuscript, then whoever copyedits your final manuscript may do simple copyediting—checking and correcting spelling, consistency, grammar, and related matters, and marking the text for composition. But if you have not worked with a developmental editor, a copyeditor coming to your unedited manuscript may, at your request, do anything from a very deep editing of your work—which might involve radical revision and your subsequent rewrite—to a light cosmetic job to make sure the work is superficially correct, with no glaring spelling or grammatical errors. In any case, you as the author will go back and forth with the copyeditor until the manuscript has again been finished, this time ready for composition into book pages.

Composition and Production

In this period, you will also be designing, costing, and pricing the book, and developing specifications for such matters as type, paper, bindings, and colors to be followed by the book's compositor and then manufacturer. You will also be preparing a design and writing selling copy for the cover, whether you are going to be publishing a hardcover book with a separate dust jacket or a paperback with copy on its front and back covers. In dealing with these complicated matters, you will profit greatly by working with a competent book designer, whether a freelancer you employ or a designer associated with the firm that manufactures your books. As with editing, you may do it all yourself, but the results can be very disappointing, for professional book preparation involves several kinds of high skills that you are un-likely to have.

If you are using a computerized desktop publishing system, you may have designed some elements of your book much earlier. You may actually have been doing the composition of the book as you or a typist typed your work into the computer and coded it for your de-sired format. But whether you use a typewriter, a simple computerized word-processing system, or the latest set of desktop-publishing sys-tems, and whether you hire expert help or do it yourself, these edit-ing and design functions must be performed if the final result is to be a professional-looking book.

However it gets there, your manuscript—now copyedited and coded—will be in a computer's memory. The computer may even be ready to produce camera-ready copy—that is, copy used to make plates for use in printing machines. You as the author will now read the book, either on paper or on screen, and either directly in page form or first in the form of galleys, which are columns not yet made up into pages. At this stage, you will make any final changes or cor-rections, reading your work both for meaning and for typographical errors. At this stage, you may also employ a proofreader, for it is very hard for even seasoned professional writers to see typographical errors in their own work. Try not to worry about those kinds of errors too much: after passing through many sets of hands and eyes, the odds still are that, in at least one of your books, you will be horrified to find one or more typos on page 1, or even on the cover. After corrections are made, the manuscript is made up into pages and paginated, or numbered. With page numbers in place, you can prepare an index if your book is to contain one.

Then, unless you are yourself a professional or hobbyist printer, you will hire someone to print and bind your book. We here use "book" in the widest sense, for your "book" may be anything from a small, self-covered, unstitched, typewriter-composed pamphlet to a large, hardbound, heavily illustrated art book or multivolume work. It may be a set of unbound pages set into a looseleaf binder or even a set of cards in a box. For that matter, increasing numbers of books may not be printed on paper at all, but rather works carried in computer memories, capable of being viewed on screen or as printouts.

The result is your book—if print-on-paper, as many books as you have had printed and bound. You may also have some sheets, run at the same time, but not bound until later, if and when needed, though we do not recommend doing this. Along the way, you will also have done some necessary formal things for legal and marketing purposes, such as securing an ISBN (International Standard Book Number) for your book, obtaining CIP (Cataloging in Publication) data from the Library of Congress, and doing basic prepublication forms for the trade. Now, with book in hand, you will make a copyright registration.

Marketing and Business Handling

A book in a computer memory, warehouse, or basement may have been published, but the publishing process is still far from complete. Now your book has to be taken to its audience. So far, all has been output for the author-publisher. Now it is time to recoup cash expenditures, get some return for time expended, and perhaps some profit besides, to serve as capital for the development of other self-published books.

For author-publishers, real marketing should start between the time the manuscript is finished and the production of finished books, while the book is being copyedited, composed, and manufactured. Earlier, you run the twin risks of distraction and premature promotion that wastes time, money, and contacts. Later—after production—it may be too late to make any serious approach to some potentially very valuable prepublication review media and subsidiary rights sales possibilities. Earlier, as the book is being written, you may be revising themes and content, and therefore audience appeal. Now, with manuscript in hand, you are able to think about your audiences very clearly and to develop promotional approaches and materials aimed directly at them.

Before publication, self-publishers, like commercial publishers, should try to produce sets of softbound page proofs to be sent to several reviewers who will only review copies received before publication. Prepublication timing is important, because they review primarily for the book trade, which relies to some extent on their evaluation in stocking forthcoming books for sale to the trade and to the public. Prepublication bound proofs should also go to several other reviewers and to those book clubs that might be interested in buying your book.

While their books are being composed and manufactured, self-publishers should also be preparing press releases and advertising copy, and securing lists of those to whom review copies and press releases will be sent. Commercial publishers, selling a whole list of books, often place advertisements well in advance of the publication of their spring, autumn, and winter "lines." However, an author self-publishing a single book is wise to prepare ads, but not to place them until the book is physically in hand. Many things can happen to a book during production, and to spend advertising money selling a book that nobody yet has for sale is a waste of often irreplaceable marketing money.

Once the book is successfully off the press, there are many things to do. Review copies must be sent from a small supply you have had rushed from the printer; such copies should go out to reviewers within days of manufacture.

There are press releases to be sent, announcing the book; advertisements to be placed; bookstores and chains of bookstores to see and sell; distributors to talk with; libraries to sell; special lists to rent for selling by mail, if appropriate; interviews to arrange; meetings and conventions at which to speak, exhibit, and sell; and the costs of all such activities to firmly grasp and evaluate. A little later, there may be agents to see and commercial publishers to talk to. In short, with book in hand, you are going to announce publication to the world and move as actively and successfully as you can to bring your book and its audiences together.

Part of the publishing process has to do with the physical and financial handling of the books themselves. Where and how to store your books, how to bill, how to collect, how to handle the inevitable returns from booksellers, how to mail and in what packages—all these and more must be settled, as cost-efficiently as possible.

Throughout the whole publishing process, for author-publishers and commercial publishers alike, run the multiple and related questions of cost, price, credit, and capital. For authors, the most basic difference of all between publishing through a commercial publisher and self-publishing is that, in addition to writing the book, the author-publisher is also generating and financing a business enterprise, however small. That makes it necessary for the self-publisher to function as a small business owner as well as author. And, like every small business owner, the author-publisher must therefore understand and handle money and business questions every step of the way. For many, the self-publishing experience is an unexpectedly large and damaging financial and emotional drain. For others, it is a source of profit and personal satisfaction. The difference in personal reactions and situations often stems from differences in original choice of content, and therefore intrinsically different profit possibilities. More often, though, it is a matter of having thought through choices and developed cost-effective publishing approaches. The self-publishing author who thinks hard about money and watches every penny is not a sterile penny-pincher. Far from it. That author is much more likely to be someone who has decided to become good enough at publishing to publish well now, and to do so again and again over the years if desired.

CHAPTER 3

From Idea to Finished Manuscript

If you want a good book, rather than merely a published book, you have to be able to do for yourself at least what a sound publishing house does for its authors, from conception to completion of final manuscript. That is best done with the help of one or more freelance professionals.

Let us be very clear that you can, if you work hard enough at it, certainly learn how to do it all yourself. Anaïs Nin, among others, learned how to do every aspect of publishing, from conception right through to running the printing press—and produced very creditable short runs of books that are now collector's items. Many artistically successful—and even a few commercially successful—small presses have been built just that way, by people with very little money and a craving to publish.

But let us also be very clear that most authors bent on publishing their own work will profit greatly by judicious help from competent professionals at every step of the publishing way. If you are not bent on doing it all on your own, and can afford it, by all means include such help in your self-publishing effort; you'll probably get a considerably better book out of it.

In any case, as an author-publisher, you will need to be thoroughly familiar with all phases of publishing, even if you do not perform all the functions yourself. In this chapter, we will outline more fully the main steps in the editorial process, from the conception of the book to a completed, fully edited and copyedited manuscript ready for composition—or, if you are composing as you write and edit on your computer, from conception to composed material ready for makeup into pages for use in printing. The steps in the editorial process do not always occur in the order discussed here, nor is the process often as tidy as the sequence here provided. A great deal of back and forth occurs between author and editor, and the timing and sequence of editorial events depends greatly on the kind of book being done, the experience of the author, and matters of personal style and the chemistry between editor and author.

But whether you do it all yourself or get some professional editorial assistance, these editorial steps are necessary if you want to do a book that is as good as anything that might be done by a professional publisher. And you should want to do nothing less, within whatever constraints are imposed by available time and money. Indeed, it is quite possible that with such help your self-published book will be far better than if it had been done by most commercial publishers today. Many commercial publishers in pursuit of profit cut corners and give authors far less editorial support than they did as recently as a decade ago, and far less than author-publishers are able to secure for themselves.

The Conception

Experienced authors, editors, and publishers know that there is a long distance between book idea and publishable book idea. In some ways, it is as long as the distance between a fully conceived idea and the finished manuscript itself. For the truth is that any group of experienced people can come up with a couple of dozen seemingly good book ideas in a longish meeting, as can any experienced author alone. On reflection, some of these books will turn out to have been done by others (though that does not always foreclose the idea); others may be intrinsically so difficult to do that their writing and other costs are prohibitive. But even the remaining ideas always need a good deal of thought and development before they are whipped into publishable form. That is why experienced editors want as much as they can get from authors proposing books for publication, including a full written outline of the book, a description of its probable audiences, a tentative annotated table of contents, and some sample material. Some editors demand far too much sample material—up to several chapters of a proposed book—and experienced authors resist those excessive demands as wasteful of irreplaceable writing time.

But no experienced author or editor doubts the need to spend a good deal of time at hard, effective thinking about and shaping a book idea before moving to create the book itself. That is so whether you publish your own book or place it with a commercial publisher. Occasionally, a reasonably good book is conceived quickly and written in a fine romantic frenzy, but that is a rare occurrence. Far more often, the book that is insufficiently considered and poorly planned turns out far too short, far too long, misshapen, or impossible to carry forward at some rather early stage. There may or may not be such a thing as the mysterious ailment known as "writer's block"; there is surely the writer's paralysis that almost inevitably develops from working on a badly conceived piece of work.

Some short pieces may be a little different. A short poem, a short story, a brief essay may seem to spring full blown and ready to put on paper whole. They seldom do, really. Most likely the process of thinking them through happens obscurely, unconsciously or semiconsciously, and you are not aware of having planned the work that appears so marvelously before you. But setting out to write a book is quite a different matter.

The best way to go about it is to behave as if you really were planning to submit a book proposal to an editor at a publishing house. Not necessarily a large commercial publisher, where there would be an overriding need to submit a work thought to be commercially viable; you might be submitting a proposal to a professional and reference publisher, which can make money on a very short run of a certain kind of book, to a small press that has fewer strictures about profit margins, or to a university press that will publish books that are not necessarily for profit.

You may, indeed, want to submit such a book proposal to one or more publishers, if only to attempt to get a professional reaction to your fully conceived book idea. If you are inexperienced in publishing, you may want to hire an experienced editor to evaluate your proposal, whether you want to publish through others or on your own. Your self-publishing decision should still be entirely your own, but tempered by consideration of professional reactions to your proposal. You would certainly be terribly unwise to conceive a book idea and proceed directly to writing the book.

Outlines and Samples

The first substantial step is to describe what the book will be about in as little as a paragraph and not more than a single page. The book will change a good deal as you later write it, but the first clear-headed full description is indispensable. Without it, you cannot see or reach your audience, and that will usually make your book's contents far more diffuse than you would like—making it also very difficult to sell your book. If you find that you cannot clearly describe the book, then you probably have not thought the matter through well enough to properly start writing it.

Sometimes, writing a few sample passages will help focus your thinking, as will working at it from different points of view. You should not actually start writing the book until it has come sufficiently into focus for you to be able to fully describe it to yourself and others. A novelist may work with situations, fictional biographies and autobiographies, and descriptive material of all kinds, and may write shorter pieces that help the projected longer work come into focus, much as a painter may work with several kinds of studies before moving into the creation of a major painting. A historian may outline, write short essays, and develop different sets of propositions and models before starting a major work, as may several other kinds of nonfiction writers. A cookbook writer or encyclopedist may write several short pieces for style, length, and form of entry before the projected work can be seen sharply.

In conceiving and focusing a book it is also important to allow enough time to let an idea simmer and "season." An idea may be a perfectly good one, though perhaps in need of some adjusting, but be abandoned too soon. It cannot be said too strongly that in this area nothing is wasted. As with all writing, save every scrap of paper you work on, and file it well enough to be able to locate it when you want it; you will very often find some use for it. If you work on computer, save all your notes and sample drafts, and make sure you have backup copies for security. Book ideas do not die, no matter how often they are put aside. They season, they transmute, they ultimately emerge anew, though perhaps changed so much that you can perceive little more than the germ of the initial idea.

With your description in hand, you should pause to consider whether or not the book is feasible, where that question is appropriate. For a book of poems, or for most novels, the question of feasibility scarcely arises; if you want to do the book enough, you will do it. But some scientific and technical books may not be feasible for those without sufficient mathematical and scientific background, just as a book on the whole history of humanity may be quite beyond someone without sufficient basic background.

Feasibility can be a matter of practical size, as well. Sometimes, the book you want to write may be beyond time and means, like that history of humanity. Some books are very hard to do meaningfully in a compass brief enough to make them practical. Even a major multi-generational family saga, which might be entirely practical for someone else, may not be feasible for you, given your writing speed, level of experience, and available time.

Feasibility may also be, to a considerable extent, a matter of marketplace realities. If two hundred books on the same aspect of computer language have appeared in the last three years, your book on the same topic may not be at all feasible in the marketplace, for you or anyone else, no matter how well you write your book or how original you mean to make it.

But feasibility is not a cut-and-dried matter. A book may at first seem too difficult, too large, or too much like many other books, but often can be modified early in its conception, becoming feasible while remaining a book you very much want to do. The scientific and technical work may become a popular book that lucidly explains otherwise obscure matters to a lay audience and may be the book you wanted to do all along. The history of humanity may become a much better-focused work on an aspect of history that may appeal to you enormously, as a result no longer posing size or research problems. The redundant computer book may become unique and appealing with the addition of some kind of twist that appeals to a particular audience.

In this very early conceiving period, you should carefully consider your audience, unless your book is intended only for yourself and a few who are close to you. If you are consciously going to do a book that will sell only to very narrow markets, that decision may deeply affect your writing choices, as well as many other economic and esthetic choices. For example, an academic may do a rather substantial, heavily researched, densely written book for an audience of other academics and for libraries, and be intellectually, esthetically, and economically satisfied by the resulting work and its performance in the marketplace. The same work, not so sharply focused and more popularly written, may satisfy neither professional nor lay audiences, nor its writer, being too narrow for general audiences, while being too imprecise and superficial for professional readers. Falling between two stools, the book may also not do well in the marketplace.

Similarly, but from the other end of the spectrum, a book aimed directly at popular audiences can be fatally stricken by cumbersome academic writing and the dense apparatus of scholarship. For popular work, it is best to leave the jargon at home altogether, and put the footnotes at the back of the book, where they will not get in the way of the narrative flow of the text. At the start, then, consider your audience.

Intentions, feasibility, and audience in mind, you should write a brief description of your audience—those you think likely to buy the book—as you would for a publisher considering your book proposal. Since you are both author and publisher, you must consider carefully how you will sell your book and to whom. This may affect your writing and your whole decision to self-publish or not. We will discuss marketing later in this book, but as an author-publisher, you will need to have marketing considerations firmly in mind throughout the publishing process.

Then it becomes desirable to expand your basic description of the work to an outline of your proposed book. For a work of fiction, that will be a descriptive outline. For a work of nonfiction, the descriptive outline may be best organized in the form of a tentative table of contents.

The one-page description captures your whole book idea. The descriptive outline casts and thereby captures the book itself. Although it and the book are likely to change greatly as you write, it is unwise to take your working outline too lightly. Develop a satisfying working outline, one you are fairly confident of working and living with as the book develops; the odds are that your work is conceptually flawed if you cannot do that before serious writing starts. On the other hand, it is possible to come close, but not quite to your satisfaction, and then move on to write some sample material if you have not already done so. Sometimes, what has been opaque in the conception becomes clear in the writing of sample material. Many writers move back and forth between early brief book description, descriptive outline, and sample material, repeatedly amending each element as the book is shaped. When you take your book proposal to a publisher, you have really shaped your book, subject to later changes as you write it. You should do no less for yourself, if you are to be a successful author-publisher.

Feasibility, in its several aspects, is raised once again in the outline. What may have seemed like a wonderful idea described on a single sheet of paper may, in extended outline, seem inadequately conceived. For example, many writers going from brief description to full outline find they have less to say than they had supposed; sometimes a seemingly good book idea turns into a magazine article or short story. The outline enables you to organize, structure, and proportion the several elements of the projected book. Then you can see more clearly the probable size and shape of your book and whether you really have a book there at all.

The sample material you write has at least as much to contribute to the development of the proposed work as the extended outline. In the sample, you are able to address the internal structuring of one or more substantial pieces of your work. The sample does much more than that, though. It tells you—and whoever you may be working with—a great deal about your writing and about the kind of writing you will need for the work in hand.

No matter how good your planning, your writing will fail if you have no ear for the language appropriate for the book and its audience. This is not a matter of grammar and spelling, by the way, although abysmally poor grammar and spelling usually indicate lack of ear or feel for the language. Copyediting can easily repair minor grammar and spelling errors, and professional writers generally avoid getting bogged down with those kinds of problems, especially during the early stages of writing. But writing that is diffuse, unfocused, hopelessly pedantic, cliché-ridden, or so high-blown as to become laughable may be work that is beyond fixing by a copy editor. And—at as basic a level as there is in writing—the aspiring author who cannot form a sensible sentence or string several sentences together so that they make a coherent paragraph needs more help than any editor can provide. The idea may still be feasible, but the book may then have to come from its creator through the head and hands of a skilled ghostwriter or acknowledged co-author. And if that is the case, you want to know it as early in the game as possible, to avoid a great deal of wasted time and frustration.

Your sample material can be drawn from anywhere in the proposed book. Most inexperienced authors naturally look to chapter 1 for sample material, reasoning that the right way to do it is to start at the beginning. Not so. The first chapter of a nonfiction book normally states the thesis and all the main elements of the book and is therefore often by far the most difficult chapter of the book to capture in the early stages. Much becomes clear in the writing, and the very tentative first chapter you prepare as a guide to writing may change a dozen times before you are finished with the book, and it may be really completed only after the first draft of the rest of the book has been done. Instead, it is usually best to take your sample material from later in the book. Choose a specific section that stands rather independently, so that your writing can focus on such matters as tone, language, and internal structuring. This applies to nonfiction, rather than most fiction. Most fiction will depend so much on the early building of character and situation that chapter 1 is the logical choice for selection of sample material.

You should write as much sample material as you and anyone you are working with need to properly evaluate the idea you are turning into a book. For rather experienced people that may sometimes be as little as a few pages, which—along with a basic description and an extended table of contents—serves to tell all that needs to be known before starting the book itself. Many professional writers quite properly regard this early casting of the book as the most important period of all, feeling that they have the book halfway written once they have it understood and fully cast; they then work and rework contents and sample material again and again, and at considerable length, before they are satisfied and ready to start the book itself. Inexperienced authors should almost always cast the book this way, for this hard, long, and often seemingly unproductive early work can make much of the difference between a rather good book and a very bad one or between a good book and no book at all. For a badly conceived and prepared book can—and all too often does—take years of hard and increasingly anguished work until it is ultimately abandoned by its devastated author.

Gauging Book Length

In doing the outline and sample, it is valuable to pay close attention to the relative importance—and therefore the probable size—of the book's main elements. The outline makes it possible to see the work's internal structure and the relationships of the parts to each other and to the whole book. The sample makes it possible to begin to see how you want to word your piece and how many words you will need to say it.

First, you need to know the size of the manuscript page you are working with. If you are using a typewriter, your manuscript will probably average approximately 250 words per page. If you are using computer, the standard "default" setting might give you the same size page, but could go as high as 300 or even 325 words per page. Most word-processing programs today include word-counting capability. In any case, you need to literally count the words on a 4–5-page sample from your book, then compare that word count with a few pages set in the type style and size you want to use for the published book. A standard-size hardcover or trade paperback book, set in reasonably readable type, will carry as few as 300 and as many as 450 words on its average page. You will use this information to come up with a tentative page count for the published book.

The probable size of your book deserves close attention, for—from the author-publisher's point of view—words are costs. Words are time; they are also composition, paper, bindery, shipping, and mailing costs. The bigger the book, the bigger these costs. Yes, you can cut the size of a book by using smaller type, but a good book in small, hard-to-read type may hardly be worth publishing, which places built-in limitations on the savings that can be achieved. On the other hand, it should be physically big enough to be credible as a book.

A manuscript of about 200 pages, with 250 words per page, will result in a 50,000-word book, of approximately 110–160 pages, which is on the low side of the book-size range. A 50,000–125,000-word book, which is the main range for most full-sized standard works, will be about 200–500 pages in manuscript, at 250 words per page, and 160–280 pages in book form.

From these kinds of figures, coupled with your outline and sample, you can make a rough word-count projection for your book. Assuming that you have projected a ten-chapter book, and your sample chapter turns out to be 40 pages in manuscript, at 250 words per page. If that is an average-size chapter, you are likely to have a book of 400 manuscript pages or 100,000 words, well within the average range.

But if, as so often happens, your sample chapter turns out to be 10 pages long, then you are projecting a manuscript of 100 pages, or 25,000 words, which is far too short. You may not have a full-sized book at all, or you may not have developed the work as fully as you should have. Many writers write too tight, without enough detail and illustrative prose. Cast more roundly and fully, the work may indeed be a full-size book, and a good one.

On the other hand, many writers—especially neophytes—write far too long. Many a sample chapter has turned out to be 100 pages, which would project into a- mammoth 1,000-page, 250,000-word manuscript. That may be far too much book for your audience, for your time, and for your pocketbook. Even very experienced authors can run into great difficulty on matters of length of book. In one classic instance, a seasoned reference book staff produced an encyclopedia far greater than its projected size between A and F, and then found itself forced to cram the rest of the alphabet into just a few remaining volumes. Yet some modest conceptual changes and astute editing may result in a manageable book. The main need is to create a careful outline and sample material early enough to gauge the size and proportion of the whole, avoiding these kinds of pitfalls.

At this stage, you may also want to do some preliminary thinking on the possible inclusion of illustrations. Illustrations are a matter best taken up fully when you have written much of the book, for only then will you really know what kinds of illustrations and how many you might like to use, and be able to relate the costs of illustrations to their desirability for the book. If you are doing a heavily illustrated book, of course, you will probably need some very special picture research and design help right from the start. If you are inexperienced, do not attempt to do a heavily illustrated book by yourself, as the pitfalls are enormous. For other books, however, this is the time to make a preliminary assessment of what you will want, keeping your eyes open for likely illustrations as you research the work. By "illustrations," we do not mean only pictures, but rather "images," which may include photographs, linecuts, documents, artworks, maps, and more.

Seeking Outside Advice

Inexperienced authors, and many experienced authors as well, will usually find it useful to consult one or more professional editors as they develop a book idea into a book blueprint and sample. We will discuss later what to look for in an editor and where to find such professional help. The money you may spend on getting a sound evaluation of your projected work can be an excellent investment—possibly the most important investment you can make all during the publishing process.

Let us stress that such an evaluation is best secured from an experienced editor, even though it must be paid for, rather than from well-meaning friends and family. You should not expect competent evaluations from other authors or from local English teachers unless they are also experienced book editors. It is also wise to avoid agents who advertise such evaluations for fees, sometimes with a promise to refund the fee out of royalty advances if the agent agrees to represent your book and then places it with a publisher. In such situations, the quality of the evaluation tendered must inevitably be suspect. Even more suspect is the kind of evaluation offered by a vanity publisher, who may tell you that your work is eminently publishable in order to secure a profitable contract to do your book. Get a reputable, tough, helpful editor early. Real help is what you need, not misleading, ego-satisfying, self-interested, bad advice.

With or without the help of an experienced editor, it is critically important in this early period to work and rework the idea, outline, and sample material, building an increasingly clearer view of your projected book and then to pause, for as long as seems right, to make a thoroughly informed decision about whether or not to go ahead and write the book.

Beware momentum at this point. Momentum can help enormously once the decision is made and you are actually writing the book, but it can lead you into enormous error when you are trying to make a rational go-or-no-go decision. To put it as plainly as possible, most writers develop real affection for their own ideas after they have worked on them for a while. That is true even if those ideas are half-baked and the book is unfeasible. Publishers, in pursuit of their own economic interests, often short-circuit poorly conceived books. But author-publishers have no such built-in governors for their book projects. They are often perfectly capable of blinding themselves to problems and going ahead to write and publish when they should not.

One other element can affect the self-publishing decision. As we discuss in more detail later in this chapter, if the content of your projected book raises any questions at all in anybody's mind—as to possible libel or invasion of privacy—that question should be checked out with an experienced lawyer before you make your self-publishing decision. If the book deals with contemporary themes, live people, or situations that can be construed to involve people now living, you may have such a question. For example, you would not want to do a book on a recent court case or political scandal without consulting a lawyer. Nor would you want to lightly undertake a work of fiction that—even quite accidentally—deals with people and situations that a court could see as dealing in sketchily hidden form with living people, and that might be found libelous or invasive of privacy. Where the question exists, legal advice is essential, for the risks are very great.

In the end, though, after all the preparation and advice, the self-publishing decision is always ultimately yours. The idea, outline, and sample material praised by so many people—including a good professional editor—may turn out badly. Or it may turn out rather well but find itself competing in the marketplace with ten other books on precisely the same subject, none of which existed when you started your book. On the other hand, the book everyone thought you quite insane to do may turn out to be an excellent piece of work, or a bestseller or both, though that is even more unusual. The author as publisher is, of necessity, an entrepreneur, and self-publishing decisions are almost always very lonely ones.

At this point, you can still go on to one or more publishers, with your developed materials in hand, if at all possible with a seasoned agent, attempting to secure a contract and an advance against royalties. What you have really done so far is to develop the kind of full presentation you would be likely to create if you were taking that standard route. Even during and after the period in which you are writing the book, you can continue to seek a publisher. The final self-publishing decision need not be made until the day you decide to fund production and marketing of the book, which can occur long after the writing has been completed. The decision to go ahead and write without a publishing contract implies a later self-publishing decision, though. Otherwise, you are simply writing a whole book on speculation—a well-worn path, but scarcely one experienced publishing people who cared about you would recommend.

Once you do decide to write your book, matters of personal style will determine how you go about it. Some writers take every chapter or section, hot off the typewriter in the roughest kind of draft form, and present it to one or more trusted editors and friends for comment, greatly valuing the resulting dialogue. At the other extreme, and far more often the case, many writers cannot bear to have anyone else see what they are writing until they have finished the entire book, painfully worked and reworked it, and have an utterly clean final draft they consider the best they can possibly do.

If you can stand it, you may find it very helpful to pass your first few roughly drafted—but readable—chapters to an experienced editor for several kinds of comments. The possibility always exists that you will plan a book excellently, do fine sample material, and then tend to stray from planned content and writing style as you move into the book. A good editor—who knows what you are after, and is skilled enough to be able to help you realize your goals rather than try to impose his or her own style and goals upon your work—will help you check several such important matters early on. That kind of editor will check what you have done so far against your outline and sample, looking at such matters as content, length, clarity of expression, tone, and feel for the language, paying less attention at this point to such technical areas as grammar, usage, and spelling. Securing helpful professional comments two or three chapters into a book can be tremendously helpful for almost any writer. But if you find those kinds of comments at this stage too abrasive, just go ahead and write your book; the comments can come later.

Preparing the Manuscript

While this book is about self-publishing, not writing, there are some basic editing and publishing matters to bear in mind while you are writing your book. Whoever edits and composes your work, it will be best to observe a few standard rules on the mechanics of manuscript preparation:

- Make sure that you work with machines that will produce good, clean black print on paper. That means making sure that the toner or ink cartridge in your computer printer is not running low, and that the settings you are using produce sharp, clear print. For those few still using typewriters or dot matrix printers, it means using a good black ribbon. With typewriters, it also means cleaning the keys as needed. Dirty or worn type just won't do.

- Use paper with some opacity, body, and weight to it. You need not use an expensive bond paper with substantial rag content. For manuscript purposes, the least expensive white, opaque, easy-handling, solid paper you can find is perfectly all right. That will probably be a 16- or 20-pound white paper without rag content that you will be able to purchase by the ream at any stationer's. To limit the "bounceback" of light that is so hard on the eyes, avoid papers that are too sharply white or too slick.

- Editor and compositor should get a fully corrected computer disk and a printed-out, double-spaced, hard-copy manuscript. Any final changes should be on both disk and hard copy. If you make some minor changes or corrections on the disk after printing, be sure to include them also in the hard copy, as many editors greatly prefer to work with print on paper.

- When you pass your full manuscript along to an editor or compositor, be sure that the hard copy is numbered consecutively, with any leftover internal numbering carefully crossed out or eliminated. Standard publishing practice is to start numbering at the first page of the first chapter. However, if the book is organized in parts, with a part page preceding chapter 1, then you start by numbering the initial page of chapter 1 as page 2. Any material appearing before the part page or the first numbered page—that is, all front matter—is numbered in lower case Roman numerals—i, ii, iii, iv, and so on.

- Use standard copyediting marks throughout, when making corrections, additions, or any other kinds of changes on your manuscript. Editors and compositors can be thoroughly confused by nonstandard markings that may seem perfectly plain to you, but may convey entirely other meanings than you intended.

  At the back of this book, in Appendix 3, is a list of standard copyediting and proofreading marks commonly accepted by authors, editors, compositors, and printers. It is important to learn these publishing symbols and use them properly, as they are the physical means used by editors and authors as they pass a manuscript back and forth between them during the manuscript preparation process, and by editors to prepare a manuscript for composition. Whether you use a computer, employ a typist, or type your manuscript yourself—whether you, an editor you have retained, or a compositor marks your manuscript—someone ultimately will have to make the choices embodied in these marks and symbols. Whoever does this actually shapes the look of the pages of the book itself; if you want to have a hand in that shaping, you must at least understand what these marks mean, for to redo the design after composition is usually prohibitively expensive.

- Indicate any quoted material clearly. Where the quotation is fairly long—certainly anything over one paragraph—set off the quote in a separate indented section without quotation marks.

Usage Questions

Beyond matters of manuscript preparation lies the whole area of usage, which also includes some elements of grammar and spelling. A standard style guide, a usage book, a good dictionary, and a thesaurus are musts for every writer—preferably more than one of each. These writer's tools are of the same order of importance as paper and ink.

Two such style guides are *The Chicago Manual of Style* and *The New York Times Manual of Style and Usage*. You may also want to have one or more general usage books, such as Strunk and White's *The Elements of Style* and Fowler's *A Dictionary of Modern English Usage*. A writer should also have both a large unabridged dictionary, such as the Webster's Unabridged or the Random House dictionaries, and a substantial smaller desk dictionary, such as *The American Heritage Dictionary of the English Language*. For a thesaurus, an up-to-date Roget's is probably still most useful, though sometimes it is harder to use than might be expected.

One usage question that has not yet found its way into some generally sound usage books is the matter of degendering language, which has become standard practice in modern writing, editing, and publishing. The writer or publisher who is insensitive in this area runs the considerable risk of being thought sexist by many readers of both sexes. It is wholly unnecessary and undesirable to trigger that reaction from reviewers and readers who might otherwise have been well satisfied with your work. Not all humans are male, and unless the "he" in your work is a specific person or a member of an all-male group, that "he" should probably be "he or she." On the other hand, a manuscript peppered with "hers or hims" and "shes or hes" can read rather awkwardly. The solution is more often to structure a paragraph so that the question does not come up, or to put the whole sentence in the plural, "they" being acceptably gender-neutral.

Manuscript Security

It is also vital to keep your manuscript physically safe while you are writing it. One of the worst personal and professional disasters that can happen to any writer is to have the only copy of a work destroyed, to see it literally go up in smoke or float away in flood. No insurance can possibly cover the worth of such a lost manuscript. Even if there were such affordable insurance, the loss would still be irreparable, for notes and research—all the material that backed up the work—are generally lost at the same time. Nor is the work itself replaceable.

Writers have written books once again after such a loss, but the second book is almost always a different book; the first book is gone, for very few of us have total recall.

Some writers keep fireproof boxes and safes, putting their work away every day as it is finished, and hoping that these devices will withstand fire, flood, earthquake, and theft. Others—and this is the course we recommend—make copies of their computer disks or typed manuscripts, and deposit those copies periodically in a safe deposit box or into the hands of a trusted friend who lives in a different place. There can still be a loss, but only of the most recent work. Most important, the likelihood of both copies being lost in the same disaster is very small. Relatively few writers properly protect their work in progress, by the way. Those who do not are taking a statistically small but personally enormous risk. Every now and then, a newspaper story tells about the work of a painter, photographer, or writer going up in flames. Painters cannot deposit copies elsewhere; photographers and writers can and should do so.

Writers who work on computer also risk losing all their work through a hard disk crash or other computer problems. For security, writers should keep three backup disk copies of their manuscript outside the computer. Then if the computer's hard disk fails, you have complete copies of all your files outside the machine and you are protected from the possible failure of one or two of your backup disks. (It happens!) For maximum safety, you should rotate the backup disks, making fresh backups on two disks each day, and leaving a third untouched. That way, if the main files become damaged, you will not replace good files with bad when making your daily backups.

When working with typewriter and paper, you are likely to retype a page on which you have made very substantial changes, thereby generating a new carbon copy that can be stored elsewhere. But when you work with a word-processing program, you are likely to make your changes directly on your computer, thereby changing the copy stored on your disk and making your disk one-of-a-kind once again. You then should be sure to generate a new, updated disk for secure storage elsewhere.

Writing on Computer: Hazards and Opportunities

Increasingly, modern writers use their computers to create their manuscripts on disk, with production people using those disks to drive the entire production process. That has become a given. At the same time, writers and editors should be aware that there are some potential problems arising from the use of computers that must be understood and dealt with.

Writers using computers for long periods can encounter more eyestrain and more neckaches, backaches, wristaches, and headaches than they did when using typewriters or working by hand. Some eyestrain is always associated with long hours spent looking at type on paper. That is true no matter how comfortable the typewriter, how easy-to-read the type, and however well chosen the paper. That many writers and editors tend to suffer eyestrain is simply a fact of life and a normal occupational hazard. But take one pair of already tired eyes and glue them for many hours a day to a screen with a good deal of light radiating from it and you have a recipe for ocular disease.

When the screen and keyboard being used are not high enough off the floor and have insufficient leg room for easy use, you also have headaches, neckaches, and backaches on a grand scale. If you are using your computer as a major writing tool, take great care to set up a system with adequate leg room, including a chair with good support for both back and arms. To avoid the wrist problems that have become increasingly common, choose a keyboard that is comfortable for you and place it at the proper height to allow you to type with your arms level, not twisted or at sharp angles. Make sure that the screen is the most readable one available and be prepared to switch to another, even more readable screen as soon as one can be found. Study the different printers available, and choose one that produces clearly readable type on easy-on-the-eyes paper. Above all, do not assume that you must settle for strain and inconvenience. If you can't easily find something you think really usable, keep looking until you find what you want. A poor computer setup can do a writer a great deal of avoidable physical harm.

Radiation hazard also may be associated with prolonged computer use. Much recent American research indicates that little or no hazard is associated with such use, but some American health researchers and many other health professionals around the world still express considerable reservations about computer radiation hazards. At the very least, pregnant women would be prudent to avoid prolonged computer radiation exposure. Beyond that elementary precaution, each writer will make an individual decision.

Many find writing with a computer greatly satisfying. And so it can be for some, as long as you take care to do a sound, structural, self-editing job as you go. Two potential problems are connected with self-editing on screen.

The first is that as you work and self-edit on screen, you will lose prior—and often better—versions of your material. That is no great problem as regards the excision of typos, the correction of misspellings, the quick fixing of grammar, and the like. But it can be a very great problem indeed if you come to the end of a chapter with only the final version of that chapter in hand, on disk, having wiped away all previous versions and pieces of versions by correcting as you wrote. Most writers have felt the annoyance and wry relief that comes upon realizing that the first or second draft of a paragraph is better than the fifth. But if that first or second draft is not available—if it has been wiped away in a word-processing program—there is no way to even compare it with later drafts.

Writers work in many different ways, and they need to develop patterns of writing and editing that suit their working style. The standard and quite correct advice for writers is to save every word they create; that is true whether they are writing longhand, on a typewriter, or on a computer, however they have to work it out technically. It is not always practical to save every draft, every page, every paragraph, but it is possible to save far more than most writers do, especially working with computers. Some writers routinely save copies of replaced sections of manuscript or the originals of heavily edited paragraphs, perhaps putting them in a separate computer file or at the bottom of a working file. Some modern word-processing or editing programs allow writers to track revisions, with earlier versions of material showing up alongside the current ones. Whether these are more useful than cumbersome is a matter of personal working style. Certainly writers should only do a major edit of a manuscript in a fresh computer file, holding backup copies of the earlier version untouched for reference.

The second potential writing problem with computers has to do with structure. People working on screen can have difficulty relating what they are writing to what they have previously written, even when they are working to outline. A piece of work has its own momentum. It changes as you write, developing internal balances and problems and a life of its own that is always somewhat different from the work you had planned. When working with print on paper, many writers go back and forth between pages, sections, and chapters, comparing, balancing, and restructuring as they go, doing the same with current and previous drafts.

Writers working with computers must find ways to do the same kinds of structural comparisons and reworkings as they go. Ultimately, it will probably be done with many large "windows" on massive screens—but we are not there yet. As of now, print-on-paper versions coupled with on-screen versions will have to do the job, however imperfectly.

Professional editors are meeting some rather difficult new problems with writers who have learned how to work on computers as effectively as they did on paper alone. Some rather experienced writers are presenting editors with clean, seemingly errorless manuscripts—right off their computer printers—that don't make nearly as much sense as the funny-looking correction-laden manuscripts they used to produce. When an experienced writer using a word-processing program produces a manuscript in which sections of the same chapter do not quite follow each other, and pieces are repeated in only slightly modified form from chapter to chapter, it is probable that the author did not do a final, careful, old-fashioned print-on-paper self-edit. It is a must and never more so than for self-publishers.

Similar problems can be created if writers rewrite portions of their manuscript in response to editorial suggestions and give the editor freshly printed (or typed), entirely clean manuscript. The problem is that editors need to have the original manuscript, with all its notes and queries, so that they can see whether or not a suggestion was accepted and how it was acted upon. If they receive back clean pages, the only way they can do that is to make an enormously time-consuming comparison of drafts. A good editor, like a good writer, needs to be able to trace the evolution of a piece of work, to compare the original version to the revision, and to back up and take a fresh look when necessary. Editors and writers working with computers need to find ways to create tracks they can follow together if their joint work is to be fruitful. As noted above, some editing programs—and today even some word-processing programs—allow them to do just that. Many editors and writers prefer to edit on paper, rather than on screen, because they find it easier for tracking changes and responses. If you are working with an editor, you always need to be sure to keep the original marked-up page in the manuscript, unless you and the editor have agreed otherwise; if you make major rewrites or substitutions, you should attach them to the original edited page.

Working with Editors

At the end, a book really is a shared work if the editorial job has been a sound, committed one. The vanity publisher who does only a very light edit in pursuit of profit does an enormous disservice to a writer. So does the trusted friend, spouse, or former teacher who "just can't bear" to hurt a writer's feelings. Without the requisite skills, they are not likely to do much good anyway, no matter how frank they may be.

The amount of back-and-forth between writer and editor during the writing of a book is a matter of writer's preference. But self-publishing authors who do not seek competent editorial help run the risk of writing and publishing much poorer books than they have really written. An otherwise excellent book can be fatally afflicted by relatively minor and easily reparable defects of spelling, punctuation, grammar, and usage. And an author with a great deal to say and the ability to say it well can publish a mediocre book that could easily have been an excellent one had a skilled editor done the necessary deep structural work to make the book more comprehensible.

Yet very many self-published books are completed without skilled editorial help. Some are created by their authors as they go, on computers that effectively serve as manuscript composition machines, producing copy that need only be given to a compositor, directly from the author's disk. Many are given to a compositor in hard-copy form, marked for composition by someone employed by the compositor, then composed and printed. Some good books are done this way, but not many. It is lack of skilled editorial help that makes so many self-published books much less than they might and should be, and marks them as amateur efforts.

For the relatively small expenditure of a few hundred dollars, a freelance copy editor should be able to provide fairly light but effective treatment of spelling, punctuation, grammar, and usage. If your manuscript needs deeper editing, a good copy editor will either be able to do the job or will be able to recommend someone who will. Whether early or late in the life of the work, the self-publishing author will be helped a great deal by working with a competent editor.

This does not mean that the editor should be given free rein. Writers have to be skeptical and to fight to make their own decisions as to what finally appears in their books. That having been said, the writer who stubbornly refuses relatively minor and much needed alterations made by a competent editor is doing the work a disservice. It is almost impossible to see your own work clearly, especially after having labored long and lovingly over a book. Yet in the finest manuscript, much still needs to be changed.

The key to success in this area is the choice of editor. You must find someone whose judgment you trust and whose approach to the work is compatible with yours. A good editor does not change meanings, but rather works hard to help the writer to clarify and enhance what has already been said. Nor does a good editor engage in destructive criticism or personalities; all that is unprofessional. And, contrary to even some publishing industry opinion, a fine editor certainly *does* mince words, putting the most devastating criticism in the most helpful, constructive way, with the easily damaged ego of the writer always in mind. No good editor wants to win battles with authors; the aim of it all is to produce an excellent book that has been written by the author. Even if the book is being ghostwritten, the aim is to produce an excellent book that entirely represents the credited author's intents, understandings, and voice.

Arrangements for working with editors are loose and various, so there are no specific guidelines to follow. Freelance editors normally submit a bill on completion of work. You would be wise to have the editor look over your material first and give you a quick estimate of the anticipated amount of work and cost, then have the editor work on a small section of the material and submit it for a nonreturnable fee. At that point, you and the editor can reasonably assess whether or not to continue working together for the balance of the project. If so, you would normally pay the editor the balance of the fee on completion of the work; if the work is a large one, you may want to stage both work and payments for control and fairness all around. If you and the editor are strangers, you should lay out the general terms of your agreement—what is to be done and the price or rate to be charged—in a letter of agreement.

Arrangements for working with writers are similar, except that ghostwriters often participate in advances in commercial publishing situations, so they would expect some sort of advance before beginning the work. Again, have the writer produce a sample, for a nonreturnable fee—a "kill fee," paid even if the work is never used—to see if you are compatible, before committing yourselves to the whole project.

Be sure to obtain a work-for-hire release from anyone who is writing or rewriting copy for you; work produced for hire is not automatically copyrighted in the name of the author, so this is—in essence—a waiver of rights in the material. Again, no standard form exists, but a paragraph like the following in a letter of agreement signed by both you and the other party should cover the situation adequately:

Writing produced by you for (name of book) shall be considered a work made for me for hire, and I shall own the copyright and all of the rights comprised with the copyright. If this work does not qualify as a work made for hire, then you hereby transfer to me during the full terms of the copyright and all extensions thereof the full and exclusive right comprised in the copyright of the entire body of this material.

Be sure that some such letter of agreement is signed *before* any work is done; otherwise you may find yourself in the unhappy situation of a self-publisher who has paid for work but does not own the copyright.

Appendix 1, Sources of Information, is designed to help self-publishing authors reach into such professional publishing sources as *Literary Market Place* and *BookWire* for expert help in editing and related areas.

Illustrations

Books may have many kinds and levels of illustrations. Some will be straight text. Others may carry only modest illustrations, such as a few tables and charts, which may or may not have to be prepared by an artist, depending upon their complexity and your graphics skills. Some books will have a few photographs by the author, needing only placement in the book. Others may have dozens or even hundreds of photographs, woodcuts, drawings, and paintings, all or most of them requiring picture research, technical evaluation as to suitability for book production, and skilled placement into an intricately designed book. Whether the author-publisher will be able to handle illustrations alone or will need highly skilled professional research, evaluation, and design help depends entirely upon the kind of book being done. The author-publisher whose work requires substantial illustrations but who is inexperienced in book illustration matters is quite likely to need expert help. In the long run, such help will probably save time and money, especially in the area of picture research.

Picture research is a subspecialty in publishing. That is because needed illustrations can come from such a wide variety of sources all over the world, and can cost as little as a few cents or as much as $250–$300 for a single use in a book. A superb nineteenth-century woodcut, technically and in content exactly right for the book you are writing, may be available in a printed collection of out-of-copyright (public domain) illustrations that costs only a few dollars, needing only to be cut up for use in your book. The cost of securing the illustrations will then be only the price of the book divided by the number of illustrations you take from it, possibly only a few cents per illustration. On the other hand, a current color photograph, in copyright, may cost $250 or even more to use, in the form of a fee to the copyright owner plus technical reproduction or rental fees. In between, there are a wide range of possible costs—and the need to find the kinds of illustrations you want at an affordable price.

One museum may supply you an excellent print of a work in their collection for only a $5–$10 technical and handling fee—probably less than it really costs them out-of-pocket to make and send the print to you. Another may see such prints as a source of much-needed income and charge you $50 plus technical and handling fees. For public domain illustrations in works that you cannot or do not wish to cut apart, you can hire a photographer or a local print shop to provide you with reproduction copy for $5–$15 apiece. Some picture researchers will also do such copy photography as part of their service. A copyright holder may charge you $25–$100 for a photoprint, a commercial photo supply house may charge more. But for as little as a $5 handling fee you may be able to get just as good a photo for your purposes from government and other sources in the public domain: that is, works out of copyright or works originated by federal, state, and local governments, which, by law, cannot be copyrighted. You may even be able to get what you want entirely free—costing only the time it takes for a phone call, letter, or fax—from the public relations office of a corporation, labor union, record company, or other similar institution.

There are no easy general guidelines about when to obtain illustrations yourself and when to call in professional help. Indeed, sometimes it is wisest to do both, supplying what you can easily and inexpensively secure yourself and going to a professional for the harder-to-find illustrations.

You should not begin picture research too early; you can waste time and effort that way, because your needs may change as the book takes its final form. However, once you are fairly sure about the shape and size of the book, and what kind of illustrations you want, the sooner you call in a picture researcher the better. With sufficient time, experienced picture researchers can often find inexpensive or even free images for you to use; however, if pressed for time, they may need to turn to more expensive commercial sources. If you need multiple images from a source, researchers can also sometimes arrange a lower fee than would normally be charged. Picture researchers generally charge approximately $25–$30 an hour, but their expertise can often save you money in the long run. *Literary Market Place* (see Appendix 1, Sources of Information) can help you locate a picture researcher.

When you do secure illustrations yourself, be sure to consult someone who knows a good deal about pictures, print, and paper to assess whether or not the selected illustrations are suitable for reproduction in your book. That is a matter not simply of the sharpness of the print, but also of how each print will reproduce on your chosen book paper. In turn, your choice of paper greatly affects the production cost of your book. Securing good advice on illustrations can be vital.

An experienced book designer is your best advisor on this. The earlier the consultation the better, for the high costs of securing some kinds of illustrations and of producing a heavily illustrated book may deeply affect the entire course of writing, producing, and selling your books. At the most basic, you may not be able to afford to publish some kinds of heavily illustrated books. Even if you do have or can find the money to do so, you may ultimately decide not to for pricing and selling reasons. A heavily illustrated book, done in the short production runs that characterize most self-publishing, is usually so expensive to create that a self-publisher cannot price it low enough to be able to sell very many.

It is possible, however, to do a book that is quite satisfactorily illustrated at an affordable cost, and to be able to price and sell it profitably and in adequate quantity. Illustrations can be grouped, with perhaps a single 8–32-page section bound into the center of your book. Expensive-to-secure illustrations can, for many books, be replaced by equally suitable and far less expensive illustrations in the public domain. You will probably want to do at least enough research in picture sources so you can talk with a skilled researcher intelligently and direct research efforts. You will almost always want to work with a skilled book designer early enough to be able to make informed decisions as to the quality and quantity of the illustrations you will place in your book, so that you can make the right costing, publishing, and marketing decisions.

Libel and Invasion of Privacy

At this stage, also, you should review your work for potential libel or invasion of privacy problems. In a terribly litigious society, writers must be very much aware of the hazards created by lawsuits directed against them. Such lawsuits are now often initiated on what to many writers seem the flimsiest of bases, yet a lost suit for libel or invasion of privacy—or, in some instances, even the legal costs connected with a *successful* defense against such a lawsuit—can mean financial ruin.

Let us be very clear that what follows here is not a treatise on copyright, libel, and invasion of privacy law. Far from it. Our aim is to provide only the most basic set of comments and to strongly urge you to behave most conservatively in these areas. It is not enough to have a good case that lawyers may win for you if somebody sues. What you want to avoid is having to hire lawyers to defend you. A large publisher regards the cost of defending such lawsuits as part of the cost of doing business, but a small self-publisher can be ruined by the legal costs attending defense of such a lawsuit, even if that defense is successful and the one who sues gains absolutely nothing from it. Even if you win, you cannot depend upon a judge or jury to award you legal costs, so success may not be success at all, but the worst kind of failure. The right question to ask a legal advisor in this area—and to ask yourself as well—is not "Can we win if somebody sues?" Rather, it is "How can we do this so that the risk of any kind of suit is nil or negligible?" The accompanying question must always be: "If somebody does sue, how much is it likely to cost us to defend the suit?"

Libel and invasion of privacy matters form a whole field in the law; there are lawyers who spend most of their careers focusing on these kinds of cases. Here we can only review enough of the basics to make it possible for you to see when it is right to seek professional advice before potential problems become economically disabling ones, and to be able to communicate with lawyers working on such matters.

A *libel* is a published defamation of character, which may appear in written, broadcast, or pictured form, or in any other form except direct speech to others. Defamation in the form of direct speech to others is *slander*. The libelous statement, must be false, must apply to an identifiable living person, and must be damaging to that person's reputation. Be careful here; so far, you are protected from actions based on alleged libel of the dead, but there is some possibility that the courts will change the law in this area in the future. And bear in mind that living survivors may be libeled by your writing, even when the main thrust of that writing is directed toward the dead. Also that by "person" the law really means any legal entity, including corporations and associations; these can survive long after the people you are writing about have died, and may in some instances bring suit against a writer. The lawyer who carries off your life savings after having successfully defended you in a libel suit may have every reason to feel triumphant. But not you; you will have won only a Pyrrhic victory.

The law of libel, while based on a single body of common law, differs somewhat from state to state, and what may not be libelous in one state may slip over into libel in another, as interpreted by the courts. Note that although definitions often describe libel as "malicious defamation" and "malicious falsehood," the modern tendency in the United States has been to interpret the element of maliciousness almost out of the law of libel, except where public figures are involved. As a result, quite innocently intended writings may rather easily be judged libelous if they can be shown as false or unprovable, and damaging to the reputations of identifiable persons or organizations. Note that it may help to be able to prove that you did considerable research in good faith, consulting in the process a number of sources, but that this may not shield you entirely from a lawsuit. One rule that has for many years been followed by responsible journalists is the "three-source rule," meaning that three independent sources have been consulted on a question of fact and all have agreed. Even that will not shield you entirely, but can help you to win or to suffer minimal damages if you are sued. The problem of lawyers' fees will remain, though; it is by far best to try hard not to be sued at all.

Writers of fiction must be almost as careful as those writing nonfiction, checking city directories if they are using unusual names, taking care to use nonexistent addresses, and making very sure not to create and speak ill of fictional people who are too much like people with whom they have been associated or who have been in the public eye.

As regards living real people, the writer's potential problems include the question of *invasion of privacy*, which can also be actionable. Here, no defamation or malice need be present, or even alleged.

Like libel, this is by no means a settled area in the law—far from it. A great deal of the hazard here stems from the rapid development of electronic means of intrusion into the private lives of individuals, the epidemic use of those means by governments and media, and the insatiable appetite of the media and the public for information and news which may violate the right to privacy. As the pressures against privacy have grown, so have the reactions of individuals and courts, resulting in a widespread and often successful assertion of the right to privacy.

A good deal of current law on invasion of privacy turns upon the question of whether or not someone whose privacy is allegedly invaded is a public figure, whether due to normal positioning in the public eye or to temporary notoriety. A politician, actor, or athlete is likely to be seen as a public figure, as may be the defendant in a murder case. But the murder case defendant—or, for that matter, any of the others—may *not* be a public figure thirty years later when invasion of privacy is alleged. This is a very difficult area, and the law here changes rapidly as new court cases develop.

What is very clear is that writers can be vulnerable to invasion of privacy actions when they harass others, steal documents, engage in covert listening, enter homes by use of deception when unauthorized to do so, make unauthorized photographs and recordings, or similarly grossly intrude into the lives of living people. They are also vulnerable when they use people's names or likenesses without their consent, although this is mainly a matter of unauthorized commercial use rather than matters of newsworthy or general interest, as when a photographer sells unauthorized pictures taken in the course of such invasion of privacy.

The main modern problems connected with alleged invasions of privacy by writers revolve around the publishing of facts about living people, which those people view as private, embarrassing, and protectable from public scrutiny. The law is uncertain and the costs of defending against such a lawsuit can be enormous, even if you win. If you are writing about people, organizations, or matters that may raise libel or invasion of privacy questions, by all means have a lawyer experienced in these matters read your finished manuscript. If, right at the start, it is clear that such questions exist, discuss the projected work with an experienced lawyer before you start writing, so that you can avoid problems as you go; you may even decide not to proceed at all if the hazards are too great. These are sound procedures whether you are self-publishing or being published by another. You should not rely upon a publisher's lawyer to protect you, for the publisher's needs and yours may be very different. What is an acceptable risk of litigation cost to a large publisher may be totally unacceptable to an author, whose contractual obligation to share the costs of defending lawsuits may become a ruinous burden.

Self-publishing authors should also insure themselves against libel and invasion of privacy actions. An increasing number of companies issue such insurance with reasonably affordable premiums. Some companies even routinely include libel—but not necessarily invasion of privacy—in their homeowner's liability insurance policies, as part of a quite inexpensive optional addition to standard general policies covering many kinds of potential liabilities. Should your broker not have an appropriate policy to offer, the Author's Guild (see Appendix 1, Sources of Information) should be able to supply the names of companies that do offer such coverage.

Permissions and Copyrights

All permissions to quote the work of others should be secured before the finally copyedited manuscript is put into composition. Where copyright holders are unwilling to grant requested permissions, or want permissions fees that are higher than you are willing to pay, you may want to write fresh copy in the place of the foregone quote, or otherwise adjust the copy so that the quotation is no longer needed. That is usually very easy to do in manuscript, but sometimes rather expensive to do after composition has begun. Don't merely paraphrase a quote; that can be seen as a copyright infringement.

When you do want to quote the work of others, the safest assumption to make is that you will have to secure written permission to do so, no matter how short the quote may be, unless the work being quoted is either uncopyrightable or out of copyright.

Uncopyrightable work is that which is financed directly with public money; that is, work published by a federal, state, or local government organization of any kind. For example, a booklet on taxation written by government employees or by writers in the pay of the Internal Revenue Service or the Treasury Department is, by its nature, in the public domain. It cannot be copyrighted, and can be quoted from or, for that matter, used whole by you or anyone else who wishes to do so. The same is true for a booklet on local history issued by a city or county government, or a book on personal health issued by a government agency of any kind. That includes illustrations; for example, the Works Progress Administration (WPA) photographs of the 1930s continue to be a wonderful source of excellent illustrations for generation after generation of authors and picture researchers. Do be careful, though, about copyrighted material included in government publications with attribution to the copyright holder. If you see that something included in a government publication is protected by copyright, then you must get permission to quote or reproduce it.

Out-of-copyright work is material that has been copyrighted, but has run through its copyright period. Until January 1, 1978, when a new U.S. copyright law went into effect, copyrights in the United States lasted for an initial period of 28 years, were renewable for 28 years more, and then ended, with the copyrighted work then going into the public domain. But for some years before the 1978 law went into effect, a series of extensions were grafted onto the law by Congress, with the first period remaining the same, but the renewal period steadily lengthening. With the new law in 1998, the standard extension or renewal period became 67 years. Therefore, when copyrights have not been renewed after the first 28-year period, they have expired. But when they have been renewed, the total period has become 28 plus 67, a total of 95 years. Copyright length for a living author is the life of the author plus 70 years.

Some copyrights were not renewed after the first 28-year period; most were. Therefore, a proper working assumption is that all works published in the United States 95 years or more before publication of your work are in the public domain, including the illustrations. A book published in 1999 may therefore safely use work published in 1904 or earlier. To find out if a work was or was not renewed after its initial 28-year term, you can check the annual federal copyright register, which is available in some major libraries, or query the federal copyright office in Washington (see "Copyright Registration and Related Matters" later in this chapter for address and website), as to whether the work is in copyright. A small fee will be charged if the copyright office researches a title for you. Note, however, that changes may occur in the copyright law at any time. Be sure to check that status of copyrights at the time when you are actually publishing your book.

How long a quotation must be before you need ask for permission to quote is quite unclear in this period. The law is in considerable conflict and flux in this area, and prudence is very much in order here. To quote even just a few words of a poem or song, you need to get permission from the copyright owner. You may quote as little as a short sentence from a work of prose and need to get permission. On the other hand, you may quote a whole paragraph from a different work of prose—and appear before a different judge, in a different jurisdiction—and be judged safely in the area of "fair use," where material can be used without infringing on copyright and therefore with no permission necessary. What constitutes fair use is a matter of enormous debate; you will be wise to be cautious in this area.

As a practical matter, defending a lawsuit for copyright infringement is likely to be far more expensive than the permissions costs for any quote or combination of quotes you might want to use. It is true that, in most instances, the copyright owner will only demand payment when the unauthorized quote is discovered. On the other hand, a copyright owner can also refuse you permission to quote at all and, if that occurs after your book is published, can force withdrawal of your book.

When you want to use a quotation, ask for permission. Pay no attention to those who advise you to quote without permission because your quote is brief or because the quote is likely to slip by unperceived by the copyright owner. In very practical terms, it is wise for the self-publishing author to ask for permission to quote anything in copyright and to behave as if, in this context, the doctrine of "fair use" did not exist, when quoting anything more than a phrase or very short sentence from a work of prose, and to ask for permission for anything at all quoted from a work of poetry or song. It is also wise to acknowledge the source of any quote or paraphrased quote you use, whether or not you have asked permission to use it, to avoid any possibility of charges of plagiarism. You should also keep careful records of all permission requests and responses.

Here is a sample permission letter. Note that it should include basic publishing information about your book, including the intended market, and the size of your first printing. You are best advised to ask for English language world rights; if you later want to sell your book to non-English-speaking countries, you can always request permission for those rights. Some publishers will send you a form to fill out in addition to your permissions letter.

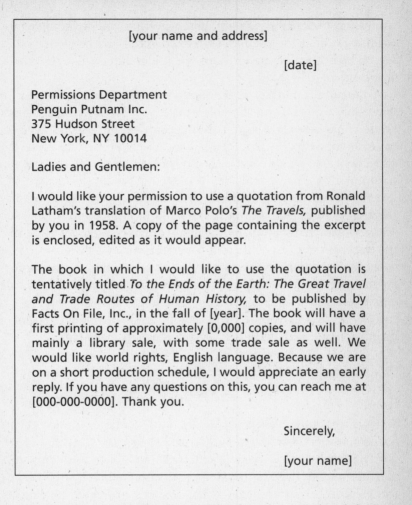

[your name and address]

[date]

Permissions Department
Penguin Putnam Inc.
375 Hudson Street
New York, NY 10014

Ladies and Gentlemen:

I would like your permission to use a quotation from Ronald Latham's translation of Marco Polo's *The Travels,* published by you in 1958. A copy of the page containing the excerpt is enclosed, edited as it would appear.

The book in which I would like to use the quotation is tentatively titled *To the Ends of the Earth: The Great Travel and Trade Routes of Human History,* to be published by Facts On File, Inc., in the fall of [year]. The book will have a first printing of approximately [0,000] copies, and will have mainly a library sale, with some trade sale as well. We would like world rights, English language. Because we are on a short production schedule, I would appreciate an early reply. If you have any questions on this, you can reach me at [000-000-0000]. Thank you.

Sincerely,

[your name]

Some permissions will be granted for the asking, and with little or no charge, especially when you explain in your letter that you are a self-publishing author. Many academic publishers, for example, will waive permissions fees, or will ask for as little as $10 or perhaps a copy of the book for a modest quotation. Some permissions, however, may cost as much as $50–$100 when they must be secured from profit-conscious commercial publishers for whom permissions are viewed as part of a subsidiary rights "profit center." That is one reason to seek permissions as soon as you are quite sure that you are going to use them, right after the completion of manuscript and before copyediting. A high fee may cause you to reconsider and change the manuscript accordingly.

You also may find that some desired permissions are hard and even impossible to secure, not because of cost, but because the copyright holder is inaccessible. Most publishing contracts provide for reversion of rights to authors when a book goes out of print. When that has happened, finding the author or copyright owner can become extraordinarily difficult, especially if it occurred many years ago. Publishers may not have a former author's current addresses or may themselves have gone out of business, so your letters may reach no one who can grant permission. When that happens, and you are sure the work you want to quote is in copyright, it may be wise to change your plans and not use the quote. On the other hand, if the quote is central enough, you may want to take a modest risk and use the quote, hoping that any aggrieved copyright holder who later appears will be satisfied by your show of due diligence in trying to secure a permission and perhaps by a modest permissions payment.

Indexing

When the manuscript has been completed, copyedited, and is ready for composition, nonfiction author-publishers can begin to face the question of the index. Some nonfiction works, such as dictionaries, may not require indexes, but most nonfiction is much enhanced by the presence of an adequate index, and is really quite incomplete without one.

There are basically two kinds of indexes. The first is a simple key-word index, which picks up those words and phrases you consider important and lists them in alphabetical order, with the pages on which they appear. You may do a single key-word index that includes all such words and phrases; or you may break out some subgroups into separate indexes, as by subject, place name, and the names of persons included in your book.

The second kind of index is thematic, in which key words and phrases are grouped by subject or theme within the index. Because a single key word or phrase appears in several subject areas, such an index is considerably longer and more complex.

Indexing is very much a specialty in publishing, and an experienced indexer—such as one from the listings in *Literary Market Place*—is quite likely to produce a far better index than you will on your own, however careful you may be. The indexer will work directly from composed pages after composition and page numbering are completed, as that is by far the most efficient way to proceed. If you identify key words and phrases before pages have been numbered, you then must go back and attach numbers to those words and phrases when final page numbers become available. But if you wait until numbering is done, indexing can be done as a single unified process.

Alternatively, you can do the index yourself, as very many self-publishing authors do, especially if you plan to include only one or more simple key-word indexes. Using a professional indexer is not as centrally important as working with an experienced editor, and many an author has chosen to save money by doing the index, even though the result will be not as good.

If you do the index yourself, you may be wise not to wait until you have composed pages, even though starting earlier is somewhat less efficient. Most inexperienced author-indexers need more time to think about what key words and phrases to include than do professional indexers. You can start identifying index entries after completion of the copyedited manuscript, and then have enough time to think over and revise entries while the book is being composed. Then, when numbered pages are in hand, you can run through your entries and attach page numbers to them, using the numbering pass as a final edit of your index entries. Modern word-processing or desktop-publishing programs often include indexing functions. These can be useful in handling the mechanics of a key-word index, but human intelligence is still required to make a good index.

The Elements of the Book

Your book will also include several other elements. Here is an outline of the usual parts of the book, roughly in standard order. Not all of these parts will appear in each book, or in this order, but many books will have all or almost all of them.

First are the group of parts collectively called *front matter*, or *preliminary matter*, consisting of all those elements of the book preceding the main text.

Title page. In manuscript, this is a single title page that includes title and author. In the printed work a "half title" page, which is a page carrying the title only, will often start the book followed by a blank page, and then a full title page, which carries title, author, and the name of the firm you have formed to self-publish your book.

Copyright and related information page. This includes a statement of copyright; any further language aimed at protecting copyright; country of printing; Library of Congress Cataloging-in-Publication (CIP) Data, if you have that information; International Standard Book Number (ISBN), if you have one; and identification of the edition and printing of your book. That is all standard publishing information. Self-publishers should also include the publishing or distribution address from which additional copies may be ordered. It is probably unwise to include price here, as you may want to change prices at some point, which is easy to do with a sticker on the cover but hard to do on the copyright page. The above information will all appear in the finally printed book; it will not be included in the manuscript you move from editor to compositor. As we later discuss, some of this information will be secured further on in the publishing process.

Dedication page. Usually appearing on a separate page, before the Table of Contents. This can be as brief as "To Ed" or a slightly fuller statement honoring one or more people. If you have one, keep it short and simple.

Contents. This is a section headed Contents, carrying numbered chapter titles and corresponding book pages. Take care to conform your final table of contents with the actual titles of your chapters, which may have changed during editing. Your printer will place actual page numbers on the contents page after the body of the printed book has been paginated—that is, has received final page numbers.

Lists of tables, maps, and illustrations. This is sometimes a single mixed list and sometimes two or more separate lists. How to handle these optional parts depends on the number, role, and importance of these items in your book and is a matter of author's choice. These kinds of lists can be placed in the back matter, following the main text of the book along with the index, but are more often carried as front matter.

Foreword. This is a relatively brief piece about the book, written by someone other than its author, usually as an implied or overt recommendation of the book by someone whose recommendation is thought to have weight in the book's field. The foreword should carry its author's name and credentials, if appropriate.

Preface. This is your own brief statement about your purposes in writing the book and, if you wish, how you went about the research and writing processes.

Acknowledgments. Here is where you thank all those who have helped during the course of your work on the book, either by name or as part of a more generally thanked group. Acknowledgments can very often be included as part of the preface without any kind of separate heading. It is wise to thank as many of those who helped as you reasonably can; the mystique of the printed book is such that those who are thanked often treasure that acknowledgment inordinately, and those who are passed over can resent your seeming neglect for a lifetime. Credit lines for quotations quoted by permission and for illustrations may be included in this section if they are not too numerous. Otherwise, they may appear in a separate section, often with permission notices in the front matter and illustration credits in the back matter.

Introduction. This section begins to state the contents of the book itself, often outlining the main theses of a nonfiction work. As such, it usually is wiser to omit this section, placing this material directly in chapter one, where readers will be less likely to skip over it.

Next comes the main body of your book or text, which may consist of these elements:

Part pages. If you have divided the several chapters of your book into parts, each consisting of several chapters, the main body of the book will start with a title page for Part One, carrying the part number and the title of the part.

Chapters. These are the main form of organization, each with its own title and covering a reasonably coherent body of material. You cannot expect the material to fall into conveniently similar chapter lengths, but you can meld together related materials to form chapters of more than a few pages long. Except for some novels, consciously crafted as a series of brief episodes, there is hardly ever a good reason to produce a book consisting of forty chapters, each an average of five pages long. Yet such awkwardly short chapters are found—regrettably, often in self-published books. The problem is often a compound of inexperience at editing together the elements of your own work and inexperience in visualizing how the manuscript created by computer or typewriter will appear in typeset form. Two manuscript pages may become one printed page; when that happens, your ten-page chapter in manuscript becomes a too-short five-page chapter in print. A skilled editor will solve such a problem in editing. If you choose to edit the work yourself, you should be sensitive to the problem and adjust your chapters accordingly.

For most nonfiction, many authors and editors will want to break up the materials within chapters, for ease of reading, by inserting one or more ranks of *subheads*. These serve, in essence, as an extended outline of the work. In some kinds of books, as in some law books, *footnotes* may be carried at the bottom of the pages, but this is an older style now seldom used. Today footnotes are usually carried as back matter, normally in sections corresponding to the chapters in which they appear; occasionally they are grouped at the end of each chapter. Sometimes, when there are very few footnotes in a whole book, it is easiest to carry them directly on the pages at which they occur, or in a single brief numbered listing in back matter.

Following the main body of the book comes its *back matter*, also called *end matter*. This matter, like front matter, is identified only by where it is placed in each book, that placement being wholly a matter of writing and editorial judgment. A glossary of terms or an index placed in the back of the book is back matter; the same glossary or index in front is front matter. Back matter may include:

A glossary of terms. This section defines and sometimes further explains some of the main and, perhaps, unfamiliar special terms used in the book.

One or more appendixes. These may include such materials as tables, charts, statutes, regulations, and a wide variety of other supporting and informative material. Valuable material is often placed in appendixes to avoid interruption of narrative flow or because inclusion in place might unbalance the book. The same material could, in many instances, be set in place in the main body of the book; placing it at the back of the book is a matter of author's choice and possibly an editor's suggestion.

Lists of tables, maps, and illustrations. These may go in front or back matter, as we have discussed.

Footnotes. These may go in place, at chapter ends, or in the back of the book, as we have discussed.

Bibliography. This may be called "Additional Reading," "Further Reading," or by any similar name that identifies it as a list of other writings relevant to the contents of the book.

One or more indexes. As we have discussed, these are usually at the end of back matter, though in some kinds of reference books they may be placed into front matter for ease of use.

A colophon. This is a list of facts relating to the book itself, which in essence functions as a combined summary of production information and list of credits for those production craftspeople and artists who have worked on your book, including the printer, compositor, and designer, as well as the fonts and designs used. Your printer will usually be pleased to set this up in proper style for you.

All back matter, except for the index, should be completed as part of the book manuscript, including any bibliographic material you wish to include. Some of these back matter materials will also be covered in your index, as when a glossary of terms is included as back matter with the terms also picked up in your index.

Copyright Registration and Related Matters

After manuscript completion, several editorial-related matters must still be done. All are easy to accomplish, though some may require a certain amount of time spent in filling out forms and passing paper back and forth between author-publisher and several government and book industry institutions. These include copyright registration, Library of Congress registration, the securing of an International Standard Book Number (ISBN), and completion of listing forms so that your book will be entered in *Books In Print* and in prepublication book industry listings. None of these but the copyright registration is absolutely necessary, but all are worth doing, as they make your book easy to find for those who might want to order, examine, or review it.

As established by the copyright law, *copyright* exists as soon as you write your material. Not finish it; write it. Every sentence you write is copyrighted as soon as you create it. That does not absolve you of the need to register your copyright on publication of your book; that registration is a vital and conclusive element of proof that the copyright belongs to you. But it does remove a considerable hazard that existed under the old copyright law, as to the possible stealing of your work by others before copyright was effected.

Copyright protection starts as soon as you write a line of work, and continues for your lifetime and 70 years after. For works done anonymously or using a pseudonym, protection is for seventy-five years from publication or 120 years from creation, whichever is less. (Again, you will need to check recent changes in the law.) Although the letter of the law states that you are protected as soon as you write a work, as a practical matter you must state on your work that you are the copyright owner and register your published work with the copyright office. The current copyright law is brand-new, so almost all of its many quite unclear aspects have yet to be adjudicated, meaning that authors should bend over backwards to protect themselves. As a self-publisher, you should register your copyright yourself. That is easy to accomplish, and the copyright office will assist you if your registration form is improperly prepared.

Your copyright can be protected on the articles and books you write, as long as you do not create those writings as part of your duties while employed by another or sign away your rights by signing a "work for hire" document that gives away your rights in specific works done for pay as an independent contractor. You can also be copyright protected on other created works, including photographs, paintings, sculptures, other graphics, plays, musical works, works created for the dance, motion pictures in their several screen forms, audio recordings, and a miscellany of other audio and visual works.

The first step in claiming copyright ownership is to print that claim on the copyright page of your book, including the symbol ©, the year in which the copyright is being claimed, and your name or the name of your company as copyright owner, as in "© 1984 by Mary Smith."

You can obtain Copyright Form TX, which is the correct form for books other than books of drama, from the Library of Congress, Copyright Office, Publications Section, LM-455, 101 Independence Avenue SE, Washington, D.C. 20559-6000. Computer-users who have the appropriate software can also download the forms from the Copyright Office home page on the Internet (www.loc.gov/copyright). This website also has a great deal of other copyright information available, some of which can also be obtained by phone at 202-707-3000 (TTY: 202-707-6737).

To register your book after it is printed, send the completed form, two copies of the book, and a $20 check (payable to Register of Copyrights) for the nonrefundable filing fee to: Library of Congress, Copyright Office, Register of Copyrights, 101 Independence Avenue SE, Washington, D.C. 20559-6000. If you choose to register an unpublished work, all is the same, except that you need send only one copy of the work.

It is wise to send the application, books, and check to the Register of Copyrights within the first three months after publication, to ensure the best possible protection of your copyright, even though the work is by law copyrighted when you write it.

Before January 1, 1978, the copyright law penalized errors in copyright registration very heavily, sometimes operating to destroy copyrights in instances of defective registration. That is no longer so, and errors in registration can be corrected, but errors uncorrected for several years may cause damage to or loss of copyright protection.

Just as you may not take very much of the work of others without securing permission, so others may not take your work. If your work is used without your written permission, your copyright may have been infringed upon. Sometimes that is obvious, as when large pieces of your work are used whole or in very lightly disguised form. More often, the infringement is not so large or so clear; then it is time to consult an experienced lawyer as to whether or not infringement has, in that lawyer's opinion, occurred; what it would cost to mount a case against the alleged infringer; and whether or not it might be worthwhile in an economic or personal sense to do so. Occasionally, as when someone really uses large quantities of your work, you can somehow justify the cost of what is bound to be a very expensive action. Usually, you cannot.

Library of Congress Cataloging in Publication (CIP) data is an entry prepared for a book published in the United States that allows libraries and other bookbuyers all over the world to catalog and easily order your book, functioning as a central source of information on forthcoming books. Relatively few libraries will order a book by an unknown author on the basis of simple notification via Library of Congress catalog cards. Some may, when a special interest book fits their own interests. For most, it is a useful convenience, when ordering your book, because of such reasons as review attention and library user requests. You can get the appropriate form to fill out by writing to the Library of Congress, Cataloging in Publication Division, COLL/CIP (4320), Washington, D.C. 20540-4320. Get the form as soon as you are sure you are publishing the book. Then be sure to complete and file it several weeks, or better months, before publication of your book, so you can receive the information in time to place it on your copyright page under the copyright notice. There is no charge for this registration. An advance copy of your book should be sent to the CIP office as soon as it is available, and before the official publication date, so that cataloging may proceed.

The International Standard Book Number (ISBN) is a unique number assigned to your book as an identification and ordering device. This is optional, but extremely useful, since bookstores, especially chains, rely on ISBN numbers (often printed on the book in the form of bar codes) for ordering and sales uses. You should get the ISBN before publication, so that you can place the number on the book's copyright page. A one-time processing fee (as of this writing, $195) is charged, which gives you a publisher prefix and ten ISBN numbers allocated for your use. If you publish different editions of a work, such as in hardcover, softcover, or different languages, each will be assigned a unique number. To get a registration form, you can write to ISBN, R. R. Bowker, 121 Chanlon Road, New Providence, NJ 07974, or call 800-521-8110. Computer users can also check the website at www.bowker.com/standards/, which includes much information about the ISBN and related concerns. You can also apply online, if desired. The ISBN agency itself does not supply numbers in bar-coded forms, but will refer you to suppliers who will do so.

The Advance Book Information (ABI) form is secured by writing to ABI, R. R. Bowker, P.O. Box 6000-0103, Oldsmar, FL 34677, or calling 800-521-8110. This is a very important form to fill out and return early, because it generates not only a listing in *Forthcoming Books In Print*, which alerts prepublication buyers to your book's existence, but also a listing in *Books In Print*, which is by far the most important information and ordering source used in the book trade. When someone comes into a bookstore seeking your book, but does not have your publishing address or the price of the book, the ultimate source to which the bookstore turns is *Books In Print*. Without a listing there, it is possible to lose many sales, especially if you are an unknown self-publisher.

Fill out the ABI form very carefully, describing your book and its author as fully and favorably as you possibly can, and casting its audience and subject appeal as widely as possible. Your book is going to be indexed in *Books In Print* and perhaps in several other Bowker publications. The better you treat it in the ABI form, the better it will be treated by the Bowker publications.

There is no charge for the ABI listing. Be sure to send it in six to nine months before your anticipated publication date, so that people who might want to do prepublication reviews will not be put off by thinking the book is already in print. Be careful, by the way, to set your "publication date" six weeks to three months after you reasonably anticipate that your book will be off the press, partly to allow for prepublication reviews, if any, and partly to allow enough time for shipment from the printer to those bookstores that have ordered them before your main promotion efforts are in full swing.

Once your book is in hand, you will want to send two finished copies to the Register of Copyrights, to complete your copyright registration, within three months of publication. You will also then be sending out your review copies, which for some kinds of works may run well over one hundred books. You should also then send one copy to the Library of Congress (at 101 Independence Avenue SE, Washington, D.C. 20559-6000) and one copy to H. W. Wilson's *Cumulative Book Index* (at 950 University Avenue, Bronx, NY 10452). There are no charges for these listings.

CHAPTER 4

·····················

Choices, Costs, and Prices

The kind of book you want to do, your ability to directly and inexpensively reach potential audiences for that book, and the size of the financial investment you are willing and able to put into the book—all of these things deeply affect your self-publishing decisions.

One of the safest and most logical candidates for self-publishing is the book you write as an expert with direct access to your natural audiences. For example, the professional who spends much time each year speaking to lay and professional audiences at conventions, association meetings, seminars, and college courses is constantly facing an existing set of audiences for one or more books. Such books are likely to be very easy to write, stemming as they do from day-to-day work in the field and often being little more than a reworking of spoken materials, probably with some amplification.

Your book can be relatively easy and inexpensive to produce and sell when you sell it directly to such audiences. Yours is the only book before them at the point of sale, and it will sell to them quite well as a medium-sized, nicely but inexpensively designed and produced hardcover, with such illustrations as you think desirable. You can also sell the book through ads placed in special-interest publications, especially if you are a known figure in your field. While such books can also often be placed in local bookstores, direct sales to ready customers are both easier and more profitable. Also note that the book you can sell to your own special audiences can easily be a hardcover, at $20–$30, which you can sell just as well as a trade paperback, while a generally distributed commercial book may by publisher's decision wind up as a less expensive trade paperback, paying far lower royalties to the author.

Experts' books like these often make far more money for their authors when self-published than they do when placed with commercial publishers. Consider some numbers: A commercially published trade paperback will, in this period, normally yield a royalty rate of 6 percent of the cover price for the first 10,000–20,000 copies sold and 7 to 8 percent of the cover price thereafter. Should the expert's book be priced at $20 and sell 10,000 copies—and that is a reasonable kind of possibility for such special-interest trade paperbacks—royalties will come to 6 percent of $200,000, for a total of $12,000.

Assume that the same book is self-published at the same $20 price and with the same 10,000 sales. Let us say that average revenues per book to the self-publisher come to 70 percent of cover price, because so many of the sales come as direct full-price sales to live audiences. Your self-publishing gross revenue is then $140,000. Take from that sum the cash expenditures you have made as a self-publisher, which might total $40,000–$50,000 in the 10,000 sales range (see Table 1 on pages 94–95 for some basic cost estimates). Subtracting $40,000–$50,000 from your sales income of $140,000, you are left with a remainder of roughly $90,000–$100,000 before taxes. Those are only rough cash estimates, and do not include the time you have spent writing and promoting your book.

However rough, though, these figures do conclusively demonstrate that—at least for successful special-interest books—self publishing can be a far more attractive route than commercial publishing.

In this instance, the key to success was in the original decision to self-publish in an area in which the author had expert knowledge and a set of captive audiences. Under these conditions, promotion costs are very low, fulfillment costs small, uncollectibles almost nonexistent, and revenue per book relatively high. Nor was it necessary to spend much per book on production to help convince audiences to buy. In these circumstances, it quite obviously makes very little sense to go to a commercial publisher.

Going Commercial

On the other hand, it is often possible for lecturing self-publishers to have the best of both the self-publishing and commercial publishing worlds. Should you want to move your work out to wide national markets after selling some thousands of copies in self-published form, you will have little difficulty in finding a willing commercial publisher. You and your book will then have a much coveted "track record," which can get you better royalty terms and a much larger promotional commitment to the book than you might have received initially.

Similarly, a television lecturer, such as a cooking instructor with a local commercial or cable television show, is in an excellent position to do some self-publishing. The position is slightly different, but similarly advantaged. Here there are two quite substantial ways to sell books: one direct-to-audience and one through book outlets.

In the first instance, you can sell books directly off the screen; orders are sent to a box number and directly fulfilled at full price. At the same time, it is possible, with continuing media exposure, to get store placement throughout the viewing area, however large, and to sell many books through conventional bookselling channels. You will then need to sell to booksellers and perhaps jobbers (wholesale distributors) at 40 to 50 percent off list price. You will also have some shipping costs for both direct and book outlet sales as well as billing and bad debt expenses for book outlet sales. But you may be able to sell many thousands of copies each way, even in a limited regional area, possibly providing the basis for later very substantial national sales. Your profit per book on direct sales will be much higher than your royalty would have been from a commercial publisher, even with shipping costs (and possibly a small sales percentage to the television station). Your profit per book on book outlet sales will be less than on direct sales, but will still be considerably higher than the royalties you would have been paid by a commercial publisher.

Poetry, Plays, and Novels

On a much smaller scale, but similarly situated, is poetry. No, you cannot expect to make any significant amount of money by selling your self-published poetry, but practically the only way most poets are going to see their poems in print is to publish those poems themselves. The economies of book publishing make it very difficult to publish the poems of even relatively well-known poets with more than a slim chance of breaking even; that is why so few poets are published by commercial publishers.

But poets should and will publish their own work, and should be prepared to initiate readings—solo or with other poets—at which they can sell their work directly to as much of their audience as they can reach. If you compose and produce your poems modestly and in small press runs, and do not go to the expense of organizing yourself into a corporate business, you may get back all out-of-pocket cash costs, and something more besides, from direct sales at readings and personal placements at local and regional bookstores.

The key for self-publishing poets is to watch costs. You may find your work becoming popular over the years, as you become better known and perhaps strike popular themes and styles, but you had best not spend whatever money you have on trying to make that come true with expensive book production and marketing efforts. The odds are that you will get little bookstore placement outside your home area and that even there you will not sell many books in bookstores. You cannot expect to get national distribution through normal chain, distributor, independent representative, and independent bookstore channels, either. Poetry is hard to make money on, and the small bookstore space allotted to poetry is usually taken up by the works of those established poets published commercially. Careful, inexpensive self-publishing is the answer, coupled with personal direct selling efforts and growing audience acceptance.

Some kinds of works are extraordinarily difficult to publish and sell at all effectively for either self-publishers or commercial publishers. Plays and screenplays, for example, have no market to speak of until they are produced, though some plays, especially one-act plays, are picked up by specialty commercial publishers seeking work suitable for student and community theater productions. To self-publish and hope to sell a play or screenplay is rather unrealistic.

Some other kinds of works commonly published by commercial houses are difficult to self-publish with any real hope of profit and offer only a very slim hope of breakeven. Most novels, for example, are best published through others, if at all possible. Even if you have a hard time finding a standard commercial publisher for your novel, you may be able to find a small press publisher who is willing to take something of a chance on your work. You can find many small publishers among the members of organizations such as the Small Publishers Association of North America (SPAN) or the Publishers Marketing Association (PMA), listed in Appendix 1, Sources of Information.

If you do find it necessary to publish your novel yourself, however, consider joining or helping to initiate an authors' cooperative; you can develop more marketing strength together than anyone has alone. Do not misunderstand: you can certainly publish your own novel and make a serious effort to get prepublication reviews in the book trade press and postpublication reviews in many other publications. If some key pre- and postpublication reviews are favorable, you may be able to get some distribution and both bookstore and library sales. You can also look forward to selling some copies of your novel— or other book—through Internet distribution, perhaps even inexpensively developing your own website. This particular deck is stacked against the self-publisher with a single book in the marketplace, rather than a "line" of books to sell or established distribution relationships. You may sell some thousands of copies of your novel, but the odds are that you will not and that your sales will be measured in the hundreds. Even if you place the books decently in bookstores, they may not sell well, with the bookstores eventually sending the unsold copies back to you.

Even so, self-publishing is greatly preferable to publishing through a vanity publisher. Remember this: when a vanity publisher seems to be able to publish less expensively than you would be able to publish yourself, that is not a matter of greater publishing expertise and economy of scale. The difference is that you will spend time and money to seriously edit and promote your book, and the vanity publisher will not. If you shop around a bit, and seek competent professional advice, you will always be able to write, produce, and sell your book better and with much more long-term personal satisfaction than if you had gone with a vanity publisher.

For the same basic marketing reasons, some other kinds of books also lend themselves better to publishing by others or to cooperative publishing than they do to self-publishing. In general, authors have difficulty successfully selling their own nonfiction works in such areas as autobiography and biography, history, literature and literary criticism, philosophy, political science and international affairs, and theater and film arts. A book on a general subject of current topical interest has a somewhat better chance, but even then your self-published book will be competing for review and bookstore shelf space with many other books on the same "hot" subject, published by commercial houses with marketing strength.

Criteria for Self-Publishing

Some nonfiction works can be prime candidates for self-publishing in certain circumstances. As we have discussed, authors who routinely reach people through lectures in person or on the screen are among the self-publishers most likely to succeed. The same is true of special-interest works—especially academic, professional, or reference books—that can successfully be sold through narrowly targeted direct-mail and advertising-placement efforts.

Let us take, for example, a specialist academic book. Given the politics of American higher education, many college teachers will still have to seek recognized academic and commercial publishers for their early work—to "publish so that they will not perish." And given the economics and marketing necessities of the textbook side of the book trade, academics will continue to need commercial publishers for textbooks. (Though many textbooks started out as photocopied manuscripts developed by a professor for classroom use and then picked up for wider distribution.) But an established academic who no longer has career reasons for publishing with a well-known commercial house should seriously consider the self-publishing alternative.

If you are going to publish a relatively short work, with no tremendously expensive composition necessities, for a limited, well-defined audience, then examine the possibility of selling copies of the work directly to your own colleagues and to specialist libraries around the country and worldwide. You may sell nearly the same number of copies as a commercial publisher and make some money doing it. That is especially likely if you can join others in your field in a cooperative publishing effort. One thousand copies of a $30 book sold directly or at a library discount through standard jobbers should yield you average revenue of perhaps $25 per book, or $25,000 in all. Your total costs, with all but your own time figured in, should be around $12,000–$15,000. The remaining $10,000–$13,000 for your time contrasts with the approximately $2,500 you would earn from the same 1,000 sales with an academic publisher. (Standard academic publishers' contracts pay 10 percent of publisher's net receipts for the first 5,000 sales; 1,000 sales at a net of $25 each yields $25,000 net, of which 10 percent, or $2,500, would go to you.) And bear in mind that your advance with such a publisher is likely to range from nothing at all to perhaps $2,000, so you would have foregone very little in the way of advances against royalties.

A regional or local focus can also give a book special possibilities for self-publishing, especially when it is also on a subject of considerable current interest. A general work dealing with several major aspects of the American westward expansion throughout the nineteenth century may be personally satisfying, but terribly hard to sell to a national or international audience, no matter how well and astutely written. But a history of pioneer women in the Pacific Northwest may sell thousands of copies in Oregon, Washington, and parts of several other states—and may have a chance at national distribution later if it does well regionally. From a marketing point of view, the key is to match content with the market you yourself can reach. An active author-publisher in the Northwest, for example, is likely to be able to get excellent review attention, place books in bookstores, get regional distributors' help if desired, and in sum sell a regional book as well as or better than a national or regional commercial publisher might have done.

Similarly, a general travel book, cookbook, or sports book may be a difficult uphill push in the marketplace, but when done as a regional or even a very local book, it may do very well indeed. It is not only that marketing is easier in a smaller area; regional pride and interest can enhance the reader appeal of such books enormously.

Special-interest books are, by virtue of their content and definable markets, usually much easier for self-publishers—for that matter, for most publishers—to take to market. From a cultural point of view, it may be seen as unfortunate, but a lot more people continue to be interested in such mundane matters as money, sex, power, and business than in matters of high culture, and their book buying habits show it. If you do decide to self-publish a general book, be aware that—to sell it successfully to national markets—you may have to spend a good deal more in marketing the book than you did in writing and producing it. The numbers and risks change very much then; unless you are already expert in book marketing, you will be wise to seek out and listen hard to experts in this area. Even if you decide to "bootstrap" your book in terms of marketing expenditures, you will probably have to spend a good deal of marketing money even in the early stages—unless, of course, you have an existing low-cost or no-cost marketing vehicle, such as a television show or an ongoing national seminar series.

So far, we have assumed that your primary aim in writing a book is the creation of the book itself. However, that is not always so. Many authors view the book also as a means of making money, and perhaps of finding some measure of celebrity as well; for some, money and perhaps celebrity are primary goals. If that is true for you, you might consider achieving some celebrity—and therefore marketability—before you publish your book. The lecture platform and the television screen first, then the book, perhaps first accompanying your other work and later standing alone. But if you do want to use the book itself as a path to money and celebrity, then you must be prepared to spend a good deal of marketing money to make money and build celebrity and that will be high-risk money.

As we have seen, choice of form has much to do with kind of book, as well as your ability to reach your natural markets and your available investment money. But choice of form has other ramifications, as well. The first and most important of these has to do with the question of whether to publish your book in hardcover or in paperback.

Hardcover or Paperback?

Hardcover books cost somewhat more to produce than trade paperbacks, and a good deal more in very short press runs. In purely economic terms, self-published trade paperbacks tend to be less expensive to produce and yield a higher profit percentage per unit than do hardcover books. However, other factors may be so important to self-publishers that they will make what may be an otherwise uneconomic decision and publish in hardcover.

First, and most important, hardcovers get considerably more review attention than paperbacks. Many books in both forms go substantially unreviewed, but a far higher proportion of hardcovers are reviewed than paperbacks. Even though paperbacks are coming to be more and more accepted by people in the world of books and bookselling, hardcovers still have much greater prestige, which translates into much more review attention.

That review attention can make or break some kinds of general self-published books. Favorable prepublication reviews in *Publishers Weekly* and two or three other trade periodicals can mean substantial bookstore placements all over the country, which might not otherwise be available. Favorable postpublication reviews in *Library Journal* and two or three other library periodicals can make the difference between several thousand library sales and hardly any at all. Librarians pay a great deal of attention to their own review media and to the specific recommendations made by reviewers in those periodicals.

Favorable reviews can also bring with them personal prestige; that can be enormously gratifying personally, no small matter for many authors. But they can also make it far easier to take your book to a commercial publisher—after you have sold it successfully in the field as a self-published book—and to secure a contract with such a publisher for your next book and the book after that, if you wish. Good reviews will also help you secure competent agents, make book club sales, sell foreign rights, and do all the other things that come with having a commercially successful hardcover book.

Hardcover books are also still more acceptable to most librarians than paperbacks, even though paperbacks are more widely accepted for library use than ever before. That is a matter of simple utility. No matter how well-constructed, a paperback will be destroyed by heavy use far more quickly than a hardcover. The paper cover will curl with use and varying degrees of humidity; the flat back of the spine will break; the pages glued to the cover at the spine of the book will come loose. Although the more expensive trade paperbacks are more sturdily built than ever before, they still do not last nearly as well as standard hardcover books do.

Hardcovers also work better for the reader. You can lay a well-used, well-built hardcover book flat on a table or other surface, and it will stay open in reading position. To accomplish that simple task with the overwhelming majority of trade paperbacks, you must first effectively break the spine of the book—which also dramatically shortens its life.

That takes us to a prime, wholly uneconomic reason for some authors to publish their own works in hardcover, rather than paperback, if they can. If you have written the kind of book you want people to use for a long time—if you want some youngster fifty years on to walk into a library somewhere, pick up your book, use it, love it, and be made larger from having entered into a dialogue with you—then you will want to publish your work in durable form, if at all possible.

The reverse, however, is not entirely true. Even if your book is intrinsically ephemeral—that is, composed of material that dates quickly and must periodically be updated and replaced—it does not always make sense to publish it in paperback only. Some directories, yearbooks, and tax and business books, for example, may work better in the marketplace in hardcover, or in hardcover and softcover editions for different markets. You may be able to charge more for a large directory in hardcover than you would in paperback. If you are selling to an affluent business or scientific market that buys such books primarily by mail, the economics of the book may work out better if you publish it in hardcover. Or you may have a rather ephemeral book that is to be sold to both libraries and people buying in bookstores. The economics of that book may indicate two editions: a hardcover library edition and a paperback trade edition for regular bookstore and other distribution channels.

Your basic decision is whether to publish in hardcover, softcover, or both. The esthetic, functional, and economic choices that affect your decision will also affect your choices of paper, print, binding quality, and several design elements. More on these choices in later chapters, which deal with the specifics of moving from manuscript through production to finished books.

The Real Cost of Authoring

It is the business side of publishing that is most daunting to the vast majority of potential self-publishers. For all but those few authors with publishing or very strong general business backgrounds, publishing as a business is terra incognita, full of pitfalls, each of which is perfectly capable of swallowing up the modest resources of an author turned publisher.

That can be true, but need not be so for those authors who recognize that publishing one or more books is, in its financial and business essentials, no different from going into any other small business. Then business imperatives take over on the publishing side; the book you have labored to write as artist-creator becomes, for all practical purposes, a commodity to be produced cost-effectively, costed out carefully, priced correctly, promoted and sold well, and distributed efficiently. It is also a source of profits which can be used for business-building purposes—as in the creation and publication of more books—or for other personal purposes.

As with any business, you must understand your costs. In self-publishing, the first and often the largest of the main costs involved is the time you spend writing your book. When you write a book with an advance against future royalties from a commercial publisher, some revenue, no matter how small, usually results from your writing of the book. When you self-publish, you write the whole book on speculation—with high hopes and great plans, but speculation nevertheless. You may publish the book, make a valiant effort to sell it, and—to put it inelegantly and sharply—fall flat on your face. Indeed, if your book is a thinly disguised autobiographical novel, a tract on the evils of the day, or deals with any other very difficult-to-sell subject matter, the likelihood is that you will not be much more successful in selling it than the overwhelming majority of those who have gone before you. The key here is to understand that the time you spend on writing a self-published book is, in economic terms, all investment time.

It is not so easy to put a dollar-and-cents value on the time you spend writing a book, especially if you are a neophyte who has written the book in what otherwise would have been leisure time. An experienced author can make an over-simplified but useful estimate, though, which can be revealing to newer authors. Let us suppose that you wrote a book of 100,000 words, or 400 manuscript pages, and took a total of 600 hours to produce your manuscript. That is straight, hard-driving, writing time. When you add the time spent in necessary breaks, like eating, that 600 hours will translate into at least 15 weeks of full-time dedication to writing your book, or, more likely, at least a full year of part-time work.

For illustrative purposes, let us assume that you then published the book with a commercial publisher, who sold 5,000 copies of your hardcover book at $20 each, and that your publishing contract provided for royalties of 10 percent of cover price for the first 5,000 copies sold. Your royalties were $2 per book times 5,000 books, for a total of $10,000. Your advance had been less than that, and your book had earned out, that is, its earnings at least equaled the advance royalties paid to you.

On the other hand, the book might have sold 10,000 copies, with royalties on the second 5,000 copies at 12½ percent of cover price, a usual arrangement for hardcover books. The additional royalty income would then be $12,500, for total royalty income of $22,500.

If the book had been a trade paperback rather than a hardcover, with typical royalty income of 6 percent of cover price on the first 10,000 copies and a probable price of $12.95 per book, then the royalty income on 10,000 copies would have been a little less than $7,800.

Depending on sales, prices, and publishing format, your range of income might have been anywhere from about $5,000 at the low end to about $25,000 on the high end. For the occasional—and unpredictable—very successful book, the range would reach higher, of course. In this instance, 600 hours of writing work might have been worth as little as $8 per hour or as much as $50 per hour. Assuming a median position, which is $29 per hour for 600 hours, then the foregone income for the self-publisher would, in this instance, be about $17,400. That is the roughest possible guess, but an instructive one. If you instead take the self-publishing route, and your self-published book does indeed "fall flat on its face," you are unlikely to get even your production costs back, much less any payment for your writing time. The writing time will then have been all dead loss in simple dollars-and-cents terms. Clearly, most authors, and certainly most self-publishing authors, do not write books for purely dollars-and-cents reasons; but it is important for authors to try to reach some sort of realistic value for the time spent in writing.

Opportunity Costs

Looking at it a little differently, you might try to assess what income you might have generated by other means had you not written the book at all. What would those 600 hours have been worth had they been expended at other kinds of available remunerative work, such as at your normal occupation? For some kinds of professionals, such as highly paid doctors and lawyers, 600 hours may be worth $50,000–$100,000. For someone otherwise skilled, 600 hours may be worth as little as $5,000–$6,000. Seeing it that way, you are attempting to measure roughly what business analysts call *opportunity cost*.

This concept of opportunity cost also extends to the time you spend publishing your book. What you are doing when you self-publish is replacing all the time that is spent by a commercial publisher's employees with your own time. That may amount to hundreds of hours more, aside from the cash you spend to publish your book. Yes, it may be a labor of love and well worth every hour you spend, but you should try to place a dollars-and-cents figure on what those hours are worth in terms of possible other foregone income.

A third kind of opportunity cost is more easily measured. That is the foregone income on the cash you actually spend on the writing and publishing of your book, from money spent for the paper you put into your typewriter or for your word-processing program to the money you pay for professional help, composition, book manufacturing, mailing, promoting, and all the rest. You may easily spend $20,000 out of your own pocket to publish and even minimally market a modest quantity of your own books. If you wish to do some serious promotion or produce a physically large hardcover book, you could spend a great deal more than that. Every dollar you spend on publishing your book is a dollar that is not earning for you, over the period of, say, a year from the completion of manuscript to the first dollar you receive from sales of your book. How much your dollar would have earned depends on how you would have invested or saved that dollar, but it is a very real cost to "guesstimate" and figure in.

Many author-publishers do not have all that much in the way of liquid assets. Like so many others who develop small business enterprises, they must borrow and pay interest on those borrowings. Sometimes it does not seem like borrowing at all, as when they simply extend and roll over existing debts and use credit card and bank account overdraft privileges. But that is borrowing, too, and even more expensive than when you borrow money from a bank or add to a mortgage on your house. For every year in which your self-publishing venture is all outgo and no income, you can reasonably expect every $10,000 you borrow to cost you $1,500–$2,000 in interest. That is a very real out-of-pocket cost, not just an opportunity cost.

Start-up and Overhead Costs

Some other cash outlays are inescapable start-up costs, including initial legal and accounting fees, a minimal amount of stationery, and some basic reference books. For limitation of liability, tax avoidance, business credit, and other such reasons, you will be wise to discuss the legal form of your publishing enterprise with your accountant and lawyer. You could do the necessary legal paper-filing and accounting setup yourself to save a little money, but we would recommend using a lawyer and having a qualified public accountant or certified public accountant help you set up your books. You should figure your start-up costs of this kind at roughly not much less than $1,000–$2,000.

Among the other continuing inescapable overhead costs, there are some accounting or bookkeeping fees and probably some additional tax returns. Later, if you hire any people, there may be federal and state forms to file, withholding taxes, and more tax returns and accounting fees. For some self-publishers, it will also be wise to purchase libel insurance. You should not reasonably expect to spend much less than $1,000–$2,000 a year for these kinds of ongoing overhead costs, no matter how small your self-publishing enterprise.

Editorial Costs

Many other kinds of costs are much more variable, depending upon such matters as the kind of book you write, how much and what kind of freelance assistance you hire, what mode of composition you choose, what manufacturing decisions are made, and how much marketing money you choose to spend.

The first of these kinds of widely varying costs relates to the hiring of editorial freelancers, especially a developmental editor, also called a line editor, who will work with you throughout the whole writing process, helping you shape and sharpen your work. A freelance professional developmental editor may charge you by the hour, at rates ranging from $30–$60 an hour. Others may charge a flat fee per job, ranging anywhere from a few hundred dollars for a brief nonfiction work to as much as $5,000 or more to work with you very deeply on the editing and virtual rewriting of a substantial novel or nonfiction work.

A ghostwriter—someone who actually writes the book in large part while you supply the substance of the material in the work—will need a good deal of cash for the large amount of time expended. That is likely to be expressed in a flat fee rather than an hourly rate. If you do use a ghostwriter, by the way, a flat-rate basis is probably best, for a ghostwriter is an author, and authors have a hard time predicting how much time a piece of work will take to write well, no matter how experienced they are. An even modestly experienced writer will charge you at least $5,000 for "ghosting" a small work, and ghostwriting fees often range up to three or four times as much as that. "Star" ghostwriters will very often want their names on books as co-authors, a substantial share of royalties, and fees or advances against royalties of tens of thousands of dollars. Most self-publishing authors are unlikely to even attempt to enter into arrangements with such high-priced ghostwriters.

Freelance copy editors hired to lightly edit your work and prepare it for composition may charge $15–$25 an hour, depending upon their experience and the current demand for their services. You can reasonably expect that a 400-page manuscript, running about 250 typed words per page, composed mostly of print and with little in the way of figures, will take a good copy editor 40–70 hours to do. Complex and difficult-to-read work will take longer, sometimes perhaps as much as half again as long to copyedit or line-edit well. Remember that if you want to discuss and dispute copyediting changes, additional re-editing charges will be generated.

You can reach professionals in editing and other publishing services through professional publishing sources such as *Literary Market Place* and BookWire, described in Appendix 1, Sources of Information. Such sources also list organizations of editorial freelancers, among them the Editorial Freelancers Association (71 West 23rd Street, Suite 1910, New York, NY 10010; 212–929–5400; fax: 212–929–5439; website: info@the-efa.org) and the Freelance Editorial Association (P.O. Box 380835, Cambridge, MA 02238; 617–576–8797; website: www.tiac.net/users/freelanc/). These organizations and others can refer you to freelancers in your local area. You will be wise to work with an editor first on just a sample of your book, since editors vary widely, and you need to find one with whom you can work comfortably.

Computer users may also find it useful to check websites of those who offer such services. For example, Dale Adams' site (www.editorial services.com) shows the range of editorial services and their costs. Impressions Book and Journal Services, Inc.'s site (www.impressions.com) describes the wide range of editorial and publishing services they offer, including a detailed set of instructions for their copy editors, which those new to publishing may find instructive. Another such organization that provides general information on editorial and publishing services online is Windhaven Press: Editorial Services (www.windhaven.com).

Picture Research and Other Illustration Costs

Another kind of freelancer you may want to hire during the publishing process is a picture researcher. If your book requires illustrations from other sources, you may find and secure those illustrations yourself, or you may hire a professional to find and secure the illustrations for you, as we discussed earlier. Picture research can be a very considerable undertaking even for experienced authors, and many publishers and authors alike hire professionals in this area. If you do, you will probably pay that researcher $25–$30 per hour. It is very difficult to estimate the average number of illustrations you can expect to secure for each hour of a picture researcher's work, because so much depends on the kind of material you are seeking, how much you are willing to pay for it, and how well you are able to describe what you want to your picture researcher. If you are imprecise in describing what you want, your puzzled picture researcher is likely to come up with far too many illustrations for you to choose from, which have taken far too much expensive time to secure.

Then there are the costs of illustrations themselves, whoever secures them. A black-and-white illustration, such as a newspaper or magazine photograph, still covered by copyright may cost $50–$100 for a single use in your book. A color photo in copyright may cost even more than that. On the other hand, Dover Publications and several other publishers issue many books and CD-ROMs full of out-of-copyright (public domain) illustrations; these are of high enough quality to be used as is, and may therefore cost less than a dollar each if you use several illustrations taken from the same book. Many other illustrations, especially those created by government sources, are not covered by copyright but are in the public domain; for these you may need to pay modest fees, perhaps $5–$15 per illustration, for copies suitable for reproduction. In addition, some museums charge anywhere from a few dollars to as much as $50–$75 per illustration for permission to use the illustration in your book; major museums and commercial illustration houses may charge even more.

You may use no researched illustrations at all, or just a few that are free for the taking and easy to find. But if you want to do a heavily illustrated book carrying many in-copyright works, you will be wise to hire an experienced picture researcher. A professional researcher will not only find the desired illustrations more efficiently but is quite likely to save you a good deal of money besides, even after his or her fee. Most notably, an experienced researcher will often be able to find out-of-copyright and public domain illustrations that will suit your needs just as well as the very expensive in-copyright illustrations you are likely to see first. For more on picture research questions, see chapter 3.

Assume that you want fifty illustrations for your book, that none are impossibly difficult to secure, and that about ten indispensable ones are in copyright. You can reasonably expect to pay approximately $1,000–$2,000 for the illustrations you want, including the cost of a picture researcher's time. For some kinds of heavily illustrated books, with many more illustrations, you can spend five to ten times that amount. On the other hand, you may need to spend only $200–$300 all told, if your book will need only ten to twenty easily secured, but perhaps very beautiful, classic photos from public domain archives. Note that when secured from commercial sources, permissions for photographs to be used on a book cover will more generally cost you $300 or more, especially if they are in color.

You may want original photos or illustrations for your book. If such material forms an important part of the work and you are not a professional photographer or illustrator, then the best thing you can do is team up with one to do the book. Then the book becomes a self-publishing partnership with both of you sharing risks and rewards. If, on the other hand, you want to hire a photographer or illustrator, your costs will vary widely, depending on the quantity and complexity of the photos and illustrations involved and the time needed to create them.

Maps and complex line drawings may cost out-of-pocket money, too. You may be able to do maps yourself with the help of out-of-copyright maps available for downloading from the Internet (make sure they are not copywritten) or looseleaf maps in the public domain, which can be copied at the public library and used as base maps. If that will not do, you will need to pay an artist to draw your maps for you. The costs of these will vary widely as well, depending on the complexity of the maps.

The design function also generates a wide range of potential costs. If you are doing a small, self-covered, saddle-stitched pamphlet of your own poems, design may be little more than typing one short poem to a page and having a printer set the type of your choice or just make plates for printing by photographing your typed pages or computer printouts. But if you are doing more—going from a 400-page manuscript to a softcover- or hardcover-bound book—then you are likely to need a book designer. That designer will work with all the elements—layout, type, paper, binding, cover, and all the rest—to design the complete package that will be the finished book. Often, these design functions are performed by the production organization you choose to do your book, but if you decide to hire a professional on your own, it is likely to cost from as little as $1,000 for a very simple book to as much as $4,000.

You will also need design and art for a cover. That may be as simple and inexpensive as working with your printer to cover or self-cover a small pamphlet, or as complex as working with an artist and book designer to create a hardcover dust jacket or a paperback cover capable of competing for buyer attention in trade bookstores. For the latter, freelance help is likely to cost you at least $500 for the design itself, though a high-powered, fashionable designer would charge a good deal more. Be sure that you retain the rights to the design, for use in possible future editions. The actual preparation of the cover costs extra. These costs can be minimal, as when your cover design consists of type alone or of a public domain photograph; but if art is drawn or photographs are taken specially for the purpose, the cost could run into the thousands. Clearly specially prepared art is not a recommended choice for most self-publishing authors.

You may hire a publishing services organization, usually called a production service, to contract out some or all of these editorial and illustration costs—as well as the rest of the costs right up to finished books and even beyond—or you may handle some or all of them yourself. Either way, the functions and costs are there and must be understood and performed.

The process of preparing illustrations for actual use in the book is an expert's job, and should be done by the designer or book producer you bring in to handle the physical side of the production process for you. Traditionally, this involved the very laborious and meticulous sizing, cropping, and literally pasting up of reproduction copies of the illustrations onto large sheets called *mechanicals*. High-speed, capacious computers are increasingly making such paste-ups a thing of the past. More often today, illustrations are scanned into a computer memory, where they are sized, cropped, and otherwise manipulated for use on film that will ultimately be used to make plates for printing.

Low-cost scanners may tempt many author-publishers to handle this side of the production process themselves. Our advice is: don't. The money you would spend on purchasing a scanner and appropriate software, and the time you would spend in learning how to use it, would be far better spent in hiring a professional to do the job for you. Even if you already have a scanner and software, and some experience in using it, you cannot match the quality of image-handling that would result from an experienced designer using professional equipment. Low-cost scanners are simply not good enough.

Prepublication Production Costs

Publishers must deal with several other kinds of prepublication cash costs, which vary widely with the size and complexity of the book, and with what you want the book to be, in a physical sense. A little hand-typed book of poetry may cost nothing more than the time it takes you to key it into your computer for composition. The 400-page manuscript going into book form may be quite another matter, however. There the cost will include such matters as the complexity of composition and the possibly quite substantial cost of page makeup, which in a computer-oriented publishing production world has come to include what earlier were sharply separable composition costs.

Some miscellaneous minor production costs include the questions of authors' alterations (AAs) and printers' errors (PEs), both relating to who pays for the costs of changes made in the manuscript during the production process. PEs are changes made to correct errors introduced during the composition of type from manuscript. AAs are any changes an author makes in composed type, except for correction of PEs. Above a certain allowance, generally 10 percent of the original composition cost (*not* 10 percent of the words), the author bears the cost of AAs, so any PEs should be clearly marked during proofreading. For a fuller discussion of AAs and PEs, see Chapter 5 and the Glossary.

Another cost is the creation of advance bound prepublication copies of your book. If you want prepublication reviews in the few review media aimed mainly toward the book trade, you will have to provide advance copies to review. This is normally done by providing uncorrected bound copies of the pages of your book, usually in trade paperback form, without illustrations or index, so that reviews can be written and appear in time for booksellers to enter prepublication orders. You will be best advised to include the costs of bound proofs in the package of services you negotiate with whoever is producing the book. In any case, be sure to establish beforehand the number of sets of bound and loose proofs you will be getting, and what price you will have to pay for any additional sets, if desired.

Indexing, if needed, will usually come after your book has been composed and paginated. Many self-publishers do modest indexes on their own; others hire professional indexers, directly or through their book production service organizations. Indeed, indexing and many others of the functions described above will best be handled by a professional publishing service organization, which can also oversee the actual manufacturing of the book. Such professionals are likely to be able to obtain a better price for many functions, since they have established relationships with many freelancers and suppliers. Balanced against this are the additional costs for their own time and your possible desire to perform some or many of these functions yourself.

Manufacturing Costs

Manufacturing costs are a direct function of the book you want to produce. All the manufacturing choices you make are also cost choices. One kind of book may cost 50 cents per completely finished unit to manufacture; another may cost $50. It may cost only $1–$2 a book to turn your 400-page manuscript into some thousands of smallish trade paperbacks. It may cost $5–$10 a book to turn the same composed 400-page manuscript into a run of rather large, quite substantial hardcover books.

Aside from income foregone while writing your book, manufacturing costs are often the largest single kind of expenditure you are likely to make as a self-publisher. It is certainly your largest cash expenditure, unless you involve yourself in heavy advertising and other promotional outlays. It is highly variable, though, and the amount spent will depend greatly on your other choices. If you spend $1 a book to manufacture 500 very small paperback books of poetry, you will be spending $500 on the first printing. If you spend $5 per book to manufacture 5,000 rather expensive hardcover books, you will be spending $25,000 on the first printing.

Cost per book tends to go down as manufacturing costs go up, primarily because as print runs get larger there is less handling time per book on the press, as well as other economies of scale, such as paper purchases. But total cash costs go up as more books are produced, so seeming economies of scale are sometimes only traps for the overly hopeful and unwary. You don't "save" one dollar per book by producing twice as many books as you can actually sell, in the process losing all the money you have put into the unsold books. Neither do you "save" money by dividing all your other premanufacturing costs ("plant" costs) over a larger press run to get a "lower" cost per book. That is merely the creation of an accounting fiction.

Marketing Costs

On the marketing side, there are fewer irreducible out-of-pocket expenditures than on the writing, editing, and manufacturing sides. However, you are likely to spend a good deal of valuable time taking your book to market, no matter how inexpensively you do so. You may need time to create advertising and publicity; show and tell potential buyers about your book at meetings, exhibits, readings, and lectures; place your book with chains, independent booksellers, and wholesalers; and create brochures and direct-mail selling packages, if you market in that way. All require varying levels of expenditure, but all take considerable amounts of your own time, no matter how much professional help you get along the way.

Do not be surprised if you find yourself spending hundreds of hours selling your book after you have written it and taken it all the way through the publication process to finished book. That is a cost, to be evaluated in dollars and cents, just as you evaluated the cost of writing your book. And this is a cost that, for many authors, is not offset by the psychic rewards that come from writing and producing a book. Some authors do enjoy the recognition that can come with having a book out, but one of the main hazards connected with publishing and selling your own book is the possibility that you may find yourself working hard at the relatively uncongenial pursuit of marketing, rather than moving swiftly to start writing another book.

Some irreducibly minimal marketing costs are involved in any serious attempt to sell your book. These would include small printing costs for such materials as publicity releases and a printed piece describing your book for booksellers and wholesalers. Telephone costs will very quickly mount to a couple of hundred dollars, as you make necessary long-distance calls. There are extra automobile expenses as you move about in your extended local area, selling your book to booksellers and others. Marketing and business correspondence will entail other costs: postage, stationery, large envelopes, and perhaps some typing and other clerical help. For all these kinds of functions you should expect to spend at least $1,000, if you are going to try to sell your book at all effectively. Hiring a professional publicist costs more: how much more depends on what you want that publicist to do for and with you.

Advertising and direct-mail selling are also variables, for in those areas what you spend on both freelance help and on the process itself relates directly to the kind of book you are doing and to available budgets and anticipated results. Bear in mind that any meaningful advertising and mail selling, even to narrow or regional markets, is bound to be expensive as related to the total publishing budget for a self-published book. The key word here is *meaningful*. To produce and place inadequate, amateurish advertising is to throw away whatever money you spend. To produce and send poorly done direct-mail pieces to the wrong prospective purchasers or to too few prospective purchasers is to waste your mailing money.

Handling Costs

Also on the straightforward business-handling side of the self-publishing business are costs connected with shipping, billing, collecting, and recordkeeping. People new to the book business are often surprised at just how costly it is to ship books to booksellers and individual bookbuyers. For example, your 400-page manuscript, now turned into a 250-page standard-size book, will be likely to weigh 1 to 1½ pounds in hardcover, or ½ to ¾ pound in trade paperback. On the other hand, you can certainly pass along shipping and handling costs on direct single-copy sales, as do most publishers, large and small. Probably $6–$7 is reasonable for shipping and handling costs, which is no less than you really spend when you take handling time into account.

Multiple book shipments cost considerably less per book than do single-copy shipments, but may not always include a pass-along payment back to you. Costs vary by carrier, often depending on weight, distance, and the steepness of rate increases. The U.S. Postal Service (USPS) and the United Parcel Service (UPS) have been the main competitors for such shipments over the years. Current information on rates and practices can be had for a visit to your local post office or a call to UPS (800-PICK-UPS). Computer users can also get such information from the USPS and UPS Internet websites (www.usps.gov and www.ups.com, respectively). Traditionally, the charges have averaged nearly the same, with UPS often being preferred because of its relative speed and reliability. You must also include in your calculations the cost of shipping materials.

Storage of books may or may not be an out-of-pocket cost. Many author-publishers store their book stock in their own homes. For those who hire storage space, the cost of storage for at least a year should be figured into costs. With the increase in self-publishing, more and more printers and binderies are also offering fulfillment services for both storage and handling. That is a route you may want to explore, although the additional costs and delays in handling may militate against using such services.

On the financial side, there is the cost of billing and often re-billing, as well as telephone collection efforts when rebillings have proven fruitless. If you ultimately hire a collection agency, there is the foregone income from the agency's cut of whatever collection is made. Finally, there is the lost income from a totally uncollectible account, and there are always some, in any business.

Some hidden costs are connected with credit and collection.

When others buy from you and you must await payment for several months—as so often occurs when booksellers are slow in paying small publishers—then the opportunity cost or the amount of interest must be figured into your costs. Someone who owes you $1,000 is costing you, for example, three-fourths of one percent per month, or $9 per $1,000 per month—if 9 percent is what you might otherwise earn relatively safely on your money. If that goes on for six months, your opportunity cost is $54 per $1,000. If, on the other hand, you are borrowing that $1,000 to finance your self-publishing business, then your very real cash-out-of-pocket interest cost is likely to be 1.5 percent per month, or $18 per $1,000 per month; that comes to a very real $108 in interest you have had to pay in six months.

Most of these costs, such as shipping, have nowhere to go but up. The figures given in this chapter, as throughout this book, are very general ranges, supplied only so that you will have some realistic insight into the kinds of costs self-publishers encounter and the relative sizes of these costs, one to the other. For that purpose, they have been summarized in Table 1, which shows a range of costs that might be involved in self-publishing 5,000 copies of a 256-page 6" × 9" hardcover, composed mostly of text, with 20 illustrations of various kinds and averaging a little over 400 words per printed page (your original 400-page manuscript, translated into printed pages). With luck and some very careful shopping and bargaining, you might arrange to pay less for some of these services. However, especially with little knowledge of publishing and printing, you could pay far more. The self-publishing decision—and many of the other decisions in the publishing process—can involve considerable costs and should not be one taken lightly or unknowingly.

Table 1: Approximate range of costs for 5,000 copies of a 256-page 6" × 9" hardcover, with twenty illustrations, as described above.

Author's writing time	$ 17,000–$18,000
Opportunity cost	2,000– 3,000
Start-up and administrative	1,000– 2,000
Editorial	1,000– 3,000
Illustrations	1,000– 2,000
Project management, composition, other prepress	2,000– 3,500
Manufacturing	9,500– 11,000
Marketing	2,000– 5,000
Shipping	2,000– 4,000
TOTAL	$37,500–$51,500

Pricing

All the figures should be taken into account in fixing the price for your book, although there are other factors than cost to consider in pricing. Pricing is actually done during the manufacturing stage of the publishing process, but it is appropriate to discuss it here, with the whole range of costs freshly in mind.

For the self-publishing author, pricing is far more likely to be a matter of roughly approximating the prices of similar books in the marketplace than of soberly and precisely estimating costs, discounts, needed profit margins, and consequent selling prices. The plain truth is that—once you have realistically figured in all the kinds of costs we have previously discussed, including the relatively huge cost of all your time, and have made a reasonably conservative estimate of the number of books you are likely to sell—there is hardly any way in the world to anticipate profits out of self-publishing. You may hit a bonanza book, of course, but no one should self-publish with the aim of striking it rich with a single self-published book. That way lies great disappointment—and perhaps personal bankruptcy as well. Authors publishing through commercial houses should have no illusions either; very few books come even close to adequately compensating their authors for the amount of time put into the creation of the work. But none of this has ever stopped authors from writing their books, or from finding ways to put their work into print or electronic forms, as self-publishers or through publication by others. Essentially, we write because we must.

Most self-publishing authors are quite content to be able to take their books through the publication process into print and then out into the marketplace with a fair chance of getting their out-of-pocket cash expenditures back and something more for their time. The pricing of self-published books should properly aim at those quite achievable goals, not at the profit goals that commercial publishers must seek. That can be a considerable advantage in the marketplace; for example, self-publishers of narrow-market professional, academic, and reference works need not price themselves out of some of their natural markets, as is so often the case when commercial publishers are struggling for profits that will meet the goals of their massive conglomerate owners.

That does not mean pricing your book much lower than those around it in a bookstore or much lower than similar books offered by mail or sold off the lecture platform. People buy books for many reasons, only one of which is price; a too-low price may not even help sales of your book. The main aim is to charge a competitive price for your book, rather than one so high that it may make people hesitate at the moment of making what may be an impulsive buying decision.

Take, for example, that smallish, softcover book of poetry we have discussed. It may have cost very little to set in type, print, and bind, and you may have used no freelance assistance at all, except that one of your friends supplied several lovely drawings in return for a small share of the proceeds, if any. It may be set in typewriter type, or more likely on a home computer equipped with an appropriate word-processing program. It is quite possible that you have put no more than perhaps $1,000 in cash into it, including composition, print, binding, and even the small amounts you have spent on a homemade press release, some extra gasoline, telephone expenses, and perhaps even a few small ads in a regional poetry magazine, a college or alumni publication, and a very local newspaper. For that $1,000, you may have 1,000 copies of a modest trade paperback in hand, some hundreds of which have been placed in local book outlets and the rest of which you plan to sell at poetry readings and perhaps through a small mailing to friends and other poets. You plan to make any further cash promotional expenditures entirely out of whatever cash beyond your $1,000 cash investment you earn from sales.

One very normal tendency in that situation is to price the book at something like $2.95, even after 40 percent bookstore discounts. That will yield you nearly twice what each of those 1,000 books has actually cost you in out-of-pocket cash. And those you sell yourself at full price will yield almost triple your cash cost, even though those you sell by mail will not yield quite as much because of the cost of mailing.

That is entirely sound thinking, given your very low cash costs, but it may be too low a price to charge. A trip to the local bookstore may show you similar books selling at $3.95–$7.95, and sometimes even more, which means that the market will bear a higher price than you thought to charge. And you may need the higher price, for you may print 1,000 books but sell only a few hundred. Think of it this way: if you price your book at $2.95 and sell half of them through booksellers at 40 percent off and half of them at poetry readings at full price, your average revenue per book is $2.36, and you have to sell 424 books to get your $1,000 in cash out of pocket back. But if you price it at $5.95 and that price is competitive in the marketplace, you need sell only 210 books. You may not be able to sell 424 books of poetry, but you should be able to get your money back out of at least 210 sales just to people who know and admire you and your work, and your courage in publishing it.

This is, of course, all very elementary, but it is important to see it clearly. Far too many writers habitually allow themselves to be put off by the "mysteries" of the publishing business. Those mysteries are really only very basic small business matters and numbers, somewhat less complicated than those encountered every day by the people running any local mom-and-pop small business. In the instance above, the only real business mistakes the poet can make are to price too low and to print too many copies. Proper pricing and competent marketing by reaching for natural personal, local, and special-interest markets will get the poet's cash back, and probably then some.

The numbers and necessities work in basically the same fashion for somewhat more complex and expensive self-published books as well.

Within certain bounds, however, marketing considerations have more to do with pricing than do costs. Like commercial publishers, self-publishing authors will, to a large extent, price their general books or special-interest works to suit the marketplace. A general-interest trade paperback, for example, might be priced at $12.95, if that is the usual price for other comparable books. On the other hand, a book that is physically the same but aimed at a well-defined special-interest market, especially a professional book or an academic work, may be priced at twice that, because that is the usual range for such books.

Size of Printing

Closely intertwined with the questions of cost, pricing, and marketing is the size of printing appropriate to the self-published book. Earlier we talked of a self-publishing author who sold a $20 trade paperback, mostly through direct platform-selling efforts. That author did extremely well, as the average sale of those books was at 70 percent of cover price and selling costs were small.

Now take another basic example but make the book a somewhat more general book, with the same price and 5,000 sales, but with 2,000 of those sold in bookstores, 1,000 by direct mail, and 2,000 to libraries. Assume somewhat higher promotional costs, because the work is a more general book. Assume also that those 1,000 mail sales at full price have cost something to make, even though they were to small, particularly responsive lists. (You should not try to sell a single $20 book to mass lists, as the economics just won't work for you or anyone else. Specialized narrow lists, yes. General lists, no.) Shipping and associated business costs will also be larger. Say total cash expenditures are $25,000.

Your 2,000 bookstore sales will yield you an average of at most 50 percent of the cover price, for now you are also selling to chains and jobbers, who get slightly more than the individual bookseller's 40 percent discount, and partly through other distributors, who also get their share. (For the purpose of this rough costing-pricing example, we will assume no returns, figuring that you will sell any returns later on, rather than having to remainder or destroy them.) Your revenue from the 2,000 bookstore sales is therefore $20,000.

Your 2,000 library sales we can tentatively figure at an average of 75 percent of full price, as you are selling mostly through library distributors, and your revenue from those sales is therefore $30,000. Your 1,000 mail sales yield $20,000 (full price, but it may have cost you a lot of promotion money).

Total revenue then is $70,000. With that mix of sales, your average revenue per book was $12. If your total cash out-of-pocket was $40,000, which included some very expensive mail solicitation costs, you need to sell 3,333 books to get your cash back. The rest can be applied to your more intangible writing and opportunity costs. (Remember, these figures are only a very general construct for illustrative purposes.)

Total cash expenditure		$40,000
Revenue on 5,000 copies sold		
Bookstores: 2,000 × $20 per copy @ 50 percent (discount)	$20,000	
Libraries: 2,000 × $20 per copy @ 75 percent discount	30,000	
Mail sales: 1,000 × $20 per copy	20,000	
Total revenue		$70,000
Balance		$30,000

But "only" 3,333 books still to sell can be a lot of books if nobody is buying. And $40,000 invested in cash out-of-pocket, on top of all the time you have put in, can be an enormous amount, especially if it was borrowed money. With that in mind, you will want to very carefully assess your prepublication sales and prospects, and print far fewer than 5,000 books at the start.

You will also be wise to budget promotional expenditures very carefully, doing some of your spending only out of cash generated from book sales. You can probably bring a shorter run of the same book to market, having used the same kind of professional help, for something more like $20,000–$25,000, spending the rest only as needed. You will still run the risks that come with a "big" placement of thousands of books via a single chain sale, which may be either a big breakthrough or a big loss if 50 percent to 80 percent of the books come back as returns, which are just too many to be resold.

The one thing you will not want to do, unless competitive prices force you to do so, is charge much less than the market will bear. Ruinously low pricing is unlikely to make you able to sell very many more books, and can make it far harder to get your money out. And if you have guessed wrong about the "mix" of your sales between bookstores, libraries, direct mail, and personal direct sales, you may need far more sales than you realized.

For every book, the publishing choice, cost, and price elements work together to form the publishing situation. The publishing choice is central, followed by astute costing and pricing decisions, always much enhanced by securing sound professional advice. If, after examining all these elements, you feel that your book stands a reasonable chance of earning back the cash you put into it, plus giving you personal satisfaction, you may well decide to try your hand at self-publishing your first or next book. Now to some of the main publishing questions that author-publishers are likely to encounter when going from the manuscript to the finished book.

CHAPTER 5

· · · · · · · · · · · · · · · · · · ·

Design, Composition, and Production

A manuscript is one thing; a book is quite another. The author creates the manuscript; but to create a book, the author must develop some of the skills of a publisher.

As a self-publisher, you must first understand the main elements and choices involved. As every experienced publisher knows, hiring skilled people is not enough; you must be able to speak with those people intelligently about every aspect of book preparation, production, marketing, and distribution. And if you choose not to hire professionals to perform some of these functions, you must go beyond that, to develop the ability to work the elements and choices yourself.

When you write a book, planning and outlining as previously discussed, you are in essence conceiving and examining the book idea and then moving to outline it whole, all the while knowing that it will change a good deal as you actually write the manuscript.

With your publisher's hat on, you should take a similar approach to creating the book. First consider it whole, though you only have the manuscript in hand (or perhaps partially in hand). Then examine and develop each element within the context of the whole book you have conceived. Do not confuse the publishing function with the design and production functions, which need to be directed by the publisher. That is why designer, compositor, and printer will look to you for direction, no matter how skilled they may be, and will undertake publishing functions only if it is clearly understood that they should.

The Physical Book

First, then, the book as a whole, starting with a very basic question: What kind of book do you literally, physically, want to see, to hold in your hand at the end of the publishing process?

A basic question, perhaps, but not necessarily a simple one to answer clearly. Your answer is likely to be constructed out of answers to several related questions. All of the esthetic, functional, and economic choices discussed previously—all the matters relating to audiences, funding, marketing, and personal goals—must be examined together when you are trying to decide what kind of book you eventually want to hold in your hand. One self-publishing author may be delighted with a smallish trade paperback, capable of reaching large popular audiences and perhaps making a good deal of money if it is well received. Another may feel the need for a big, hardcover book printed on high-quality, high-cost paper, to be sold at a high price to a narrow but very receptive professional audience; such a book may enhance reputation and need not do much better than break even to be entirely satisfactory. Yet another will be satisfied with modest sales and modest financial losses, as long as the book is published and is, in the author's eyes, a physically beautiful book.

In physical terms, a book is composed of print and sometimes illustrations on material, usually paper, which is joined by glue or stitching and encased in a cover, which itself may have another cover, or jacket. If properly designed, all the elements of the book complement each other, and the internal design of each element works within the whole book design. A well-designed, light, bright, and airy children's book page design will work with a similarly designed cover; it will not work at all with a heavy, dark cover, which turns children and parents away so that they may not even open the book to see what is inside. At the other end of the publishing spectrum, a strong reference book that should appeal to serious information interests will not work very well if the visual elements overwhelm the reference content and therefore the usefulness of the work. Design follows publisher's perception of probable audience.

The easiest and probably the best way for an author-publisher to proceed with book design is to look for models or partial models and seek to work from them. That is really what most publishers do when they "see" their books early on in the publishing process. Publishers are not professional book designers who build books from the raw materials; publishers are people who look at books they and others have done, and say or think, "I want something like that one over there."

If you want to design your own self-published book, or want to be able to intelligently direct the work of others in designing your book, go to the library and look at books, hundreds of books. Handle them. Look at their dust jackets, their bindings, the ways their contents are glued and stitched together, their page designs, type sizes and styles, the way the paper used holds inks, reproduces illustrations, and bulks up the contents of the book. Go to bookstores and see how different book sizes and cover designs stand out on the shelf from across the store—and what designs, sizes, and cover color combinations fade away and are unreadable from any distance.

Read about what makes a book. Buy or borrow Marshall Lee's *Bookmaking: The Illustrated Guide to Design/Production/Editing*, the third edition of which was published by W. W. Norton in 1998. It is an excellent book, made for professionals but written simply enough for nonprofessionals to understand well; and it is especially useful in the design and production areas.

Most of all, though, take other books in hand and see them and all their key elements *physically*. Then you will be able to develop the kind of feel for books and their physical elements that will enable you to work with designers, compositors, and printers to make good-looking books that accurately reflect your publishing desires.

Print on Paper

Whatever mode of composition you use, the net effect of it will be the imposition of ink on paper, as it is on this page. The question is how to make that ink on paper best suit your publishing desires.

A whole web of esthetic considerations surrounds the question of which type to use on what paper; that is some of the main stuff of the type and book designer's art. And art it is. Each book is also an artwork, designed and produced by artists, no matter how well or ill artistic intentions are realized—or are even considered by those who made the book. In this sense, the writer is only the first among many artists who work together to produce the finished book.

But underneath artistic considerations are some basic assumptions, which have to do with effectively communicating the content of a book to its intended audiences. At its most basic, a book must be set in type that:

- is large enough to be easily read,
- lays flat upon the page being read,
- is printed in ink dark enough to be easily seen,
- has enough body to be easily seen,
- and is laid not too densely upon the page, so the eye can easily follow its flow.

How large a book type must be to be easily read is a somewhat subjective estimate. At the turn of the century, average book type sizes were considerably smaller than those generally acceptable by book designers and readers today. Yet even today, many newspapers use type sizes that are much smaller than most book types, as do many mass market paperback books and some reference books. What is probably safest is to use a type size similar to those used in modern hardcover or trade paperback books, as that is what is likely to feel most acceptable to your audience.

Selecting Type

American type sizes are measured in points, with each point measuring vertically about ½ of an inch. For ease of reading, types measuring one size vertically are usually set into lines measuring vertically one or two points larger; this allows more space, or "air" (technically called *leading*), between each line than if the type were set "solid" into a line of its own size. It is the vertical measurement that is used to describe size; the horizontal measurement varies with spacing and type style, and is not used for measurement purposes. Therefore, a type measuring 10 points high on a line 12 points high—described as "ten on twelve," and written 10/12—is ¹⁰⁄₇₂" high set into a line ¹²⁄₇₂" high. This is a very common hardcover and trade paperback book type size; the other two most common are 11/13 and 12/14. The page you are reading is set 10/13, in a rather readable type, Goudy, which has adequate body for ease of reading, as well.

Some books carry their design specifications, usually in the back of the book, but sometimes in the front matter. Unfortunately, that is an older style, which has fallen into disuse. But if you do find a book you wish to use as a model for your own, by all means show it to your designer, compositor, and printer. They will be able to measure sizes, recognize styles, and either duplicate or approximate those aspects that especially appeal to you—or tell you why they think those aspects are inappropriate for your book.

Type comes in families, usually named after their originators or early users, but sometimes after their style variances. (A specimen sheet of some common book types is given in Appendix 4.) The widely used Bodoni family of modern book typefaces, for example, is a modern Roman group, named after its originator; Times Roman is another good-looking and much-used family of typefaces. You will not go very wrong—and probably will go quite right—if you select a type of appropriate size out of one of these two families. Caution: beware the trendy designer who urges you to use an unusual and hard-to-read type that is the "coming" thing; it is usually just a fad. If you find a book type hard to read, trust your common sense and use something else. If you are unwilling to trust your common sense, seek other professional opinions, and ask other nonprofessionals if they, too, find the type hard to read. Whatever responses you get, read a page or two, in several physical settings, before you decide whether or not a type is hard to read, set too small or too large, or set too solid on the page, with insufficient air. Many types that are very attractive for an advertisement, with short pieces of copy, are very wearing on the eyes when used for full pages of text.

Type size must be carefully considered in another way, too. A difference of a single "point" in the type size you use can make a difference of many pages in your book. You can adjust the number of pages to some extent with the page margins you use, but can go only so far before the book page begins to look cramped or, at the other extreme, "padded" with too much white space. The main adjusting device is line size. A 6" × 9" book set with 14-point lines, rather than 13-point lines—a difference of just one point vertically—and otherwise similarly designed, can have as much as 15 to 20 percent more pages. That is because the difference vertically amounts to only a few lines per page, but the difference horizontally is at least equally large; more characters fit into the smaller-point line.

This question of the number of pages in your book can be of considerable importance. More pages mean higher paper costs, and often higher total composition costs. On the other hand, more pages can mean the difference between a small, credible book, and a book that seems to its readers considerably too short to be called a full book. A 60,000-word book in the hands of an amateur can become a 100-page, fairly readable, but too-small book. In the hands of a sound professional, the same book can and should be an attractive, readable book in which the number of pages does not call into question the substance of the book. The difference between the two books is all in the choice of type sizes, type styles, margins, and trim sizes (see under "book size, trim size" in the Glossary). The 100-page book may be set 10/12, with small margins and a 7" × 10" trim size, the result being quite readable—but far too small. The credible book may be set 10/12, 11/13, or 12/14, with largish, but not obtrusively large margins, and in a standard small hardcover or trade paperback trim size might run anywhere from 192 to 256 pages, depending on what combination of type, margins, and trim size you choose. You will be wise to adopt a standard trim size for your book. A nonstandard size may not only cost more but also be less attractive to bookstores because of possible shelving problems.

The question of margins has another side, too. All too often, books are set with too-small margins on the gutter, which is the inside edge of the page. The page looks all right when it is laid out flat in page proofs, before binding. But binding uses up some of the inside margin, leaving the print squashed up against the binding and making it hard to read. That becomes a particularly difficult problem when your book is a paperback with a "perfect" binding—that is, a glued flatbacked binding. Such books do not naturally lie flat, as hardcover books do. Instead, they open somewhat bent. If a reader must flatten out a paperback book in order to properly read all the print on the page, that will soon break the back of the book. If you want your paperback book to be read easily and to survive its first few readings, be very sure to include ample gutter margins. For hardcover books, adequate gutter margins will suffice.

Don't believe anyone who tells you that the new adhesives being used in books today have solved this problem. They are better adhesives than those previously used, but are not at all effective enough yet to solve the spine-breaking problem of perfect-bound books. This is one of the key reasons that perfect-bound paperbacks are still intrinsically much inferior to books gathered in signatures, sewn, glued, fixed together, and covered again with a back that allows them to be opened flat, the binding method used in hardcover and some flexibly bound books. We recommend that self-publishing authors seriously consider doing their books in trade paper—but only for economy, never for durability or readability.

Occasionally, a self-publishing author has the misfortune to run into a designer or printer who counsels the very "artistic" approach of using something like light brown ink on some kind of off-white or even bluish paper, or dark brown ink on light brown paper, or black ink on some other-than-white paper. You may even be shown how beautiful such a work can be on a brochure, booklet, poster, or set of sample pages. Caution: don't do it. The reason that almost all books, including art books, in libraries and bookstores, are printed in black ink on white paper is that they are most readable that way. You can print lovely, unconventional, artistically interesting and satisfying books if you wish, but only with great care, in small runs, for very special audiences, and usually at a considerable financial loss, especially if you figure in your own time as art printer realistically. But that is art printing, which is quite different from the main-line self-publishing this book discusses.

The thickness of the body of a type considerably affects its readability. That is why typewriter type, which is quite acceptable and readable in relatively short newsletters and some kinds of advertising materials, is usually a bad book choice. The problem is that it is too thin, and especially when reduced from an 8½" × 11" piece of typing paper to fit a smaller book page. Traditionally typewriter composition was very attractive from a cost point of view, being by far the least expensive way to set type. However, the use of computers avoids that problem, producing a more standard, more readable book type.

From Manuscript to Book Production

From the book production point of view, there are now several modes of composition, all changing rapidly as applicable computer technology develops. From the author-publisher's point of view, however, the manuscript is by far most likely to appear on a computer-generated disk, with a hard copy attached. Occasionally, the manuscript will still be done on a typewriter; then it will be scanned or typed into a computer disk for production purposes.

Whatever the form of composition, some crucial format and copy flow matters must be taken up at this earliest stage of book production. The term *format* can be a little difficult to deal with, at first. It really means every aspect of a publication's physical appearance, including such matters as type and type sizes, paper, bindings, and the many small choices that go into the final layout of a page. It is also commonly used to describe any single element of physical appearance and design, so that a book production professional will be discussing and deciding "formats" with you at a time when you may not have even seriously considered the final specifics of paper and binding.

At this early stage, the formats you will be deciding upon are those that determine how your book's content will lie in ink upon the pages of your book. That means type; page layout style; subheads within the text; how words are to break when carried over from one line to another; the indenting of paragraphs; how to head and start new chapters; whether to use running heads on the pages; how to handle the placement of illustrative material, tables, charts, graphs, and footnotes; how to handle bibliographic material; and a number of other such questions. All should really be decided before physical preparation of the main body of the book. All should be done by self-publishing authors in close consultation with hired professionals. This is the normal day-to-day stuff of design and book production; you should not expect to be able to master it all for a single self-published book, or even while doing several self-published books. And it is not simple, for all the elements of design and resulting formats are interwoven.

Before settling format questions, and no matter how skilled the people you have hired, you must see sample pages that embody all the format decisions you have tentatively made. It is an expense; sample pages may cost as much as a couple of hundred dollars. But there is no other way to really see how the pages and the several parts of your book will look. You may have chosen type that looked wonderful on a single line of a type specimen book but looks awful when you see a whole page. You may have done a little thing, like accepting a recommendation that you indent paragraphs two characters only, in a commonly used modern mode, only to realize, when you see the page, that the choice here is quite wrong in terms of the appearance of the page. A two-character indent on a page of strong, readable type may make that page look as if it is almost a solid block of dauntingly unreadable type. Author-publishers, like all publishers, must lean upon the skills of many others—but the final publishing decisions are their own and must be fully informed.

Composition today is usually done by going directly into pages. Before computer composition that was rarely done, for it was very expensive to make author's changes once pages were made up; to break up and remake large numbers of pages to accommodate new pieces of copy was prohibitively expensive. With computer composition, however, it has become possible to "push" type forward or backward within a computer memory; that makes changes at the page-makeup stage much less expensive. With computer composition, the page is not "fixed" until all changes have been made; before then, what changes is only the formatted copy in the computer's memory.

Whether from a typewriter or a computer, the author should supply a clean, fully corrected manuscript to work from. Heavily edited, hard-to-read, and hard-to-compose manuscript will be classified as *dirty copy.* Also called *penalty copy,* it will generate extra composition charges and may also cause many unnecessary and expensive composition errors. That does not mean laboring to produce an errorless manuscript at this stage; there will be many changes before the book is completed, and several pairs of eyes will see more than the author can possibly see alone.

However copy is composed, there is a certain amount of flow back and forth between author and compositor as final changes and corrections are made. Even if you compose your own copy, that is in a sense still so; if you fail to recognize this, because you are using a home computer as a word-processor or composing machine, you run the real risk of turning out a book full of typographical errors. Actually, it is in one way more difficult to compose the book yourself, for you cannot see your own typographical errors as easily as others can. Your eye will slide over errors, even on a fifth rereading, while someone else is likely to pick up your overlooked errors on a first reading.

If you do your own composing, plan to print out your composed material and do a careful "author's read" of it on paper. That will enable you to pick up some errors in content that may still remain, even after copyediting, and to make any final changes desired. Quite often, some final changes need to be made at this stage because situations or facts—or your view of a matter—have changed. Plan also to have someone else, preferably a skilled proofreader, do a final reading of your printed-out manuscript for typographical errors. Some will inevitably slip through, as in every book, but not nearly as many as when you are content to do a final reading solely on your own and only on the computer screen.

Proofs

You will encounter several kinds of "proofs" during the publishing process. "Proofs," like "formats," can be a little difficult to understand early on, and for much the same reasons. There are several kinds of proofs, all of them images of composed material, and most of them look quite alike to the author.

Page proofs are copies of composed, made-up pages. Any final changes are made on these proofs, and it is here that you can check to see that any changes and corrections put in earlier were properly made. You will need a second set of page proofs sent to you so you can do this final check. At the page proof stage, you can also, for the first time, get a full view of how the body of the book will really look. This is when any final content and design doubts will surface—but only if they must; major changes at this stage can be very, very expensive, though electronic setting is making them less so.

Before computer composition, authors generally saw proofs in two stages. The first was in the form of *galley proofs*, long pages of composed type, set in a single column. Only after the galleys were proof-read and corrected was the type put together with any other desired images, such as illustrations, and made up into pages, which the author then proofed in their final form. Instead of galleys, authors today generally get *rough pages*, which are proofs of type and tables in roughly paginated form, but often without final art slotted into place. Unless the book is complex in design, that is the only set of proofs most authors see. As an author-publisher, however, you will want to carefully check final page proofs as well.

When reading proofs at any stage, it pays to carefully mark any typographical errors made by others as PE, which means printer's error; you do not bear the cost of correcting these. Your compositor will, by agreement with you, allow you to make a certain amount of changes without additional charge; these are called AAs, meaning author's alterations. The usual agreement enables you to make changes up to about 10 percent of the cost of setting the original manuscript. Above that amount, you will be charged extra for author's alterations. Therefore, be sure to clearly mark printer's errors so that they will not be charged against your allowance for author's alterations.

Note that a 10 percent author's alterations allowance does not mean that you can change 10 percent of the words in the manuscript without additional charges. Inserting changes can cost a good deal more than composing a body of copy word for word; your 10 percent cost allowance is likely to mean, in practice, that you should not plan to change more than 3 to 4 percent of the words in the manuscript without incurring extra charges. But you will be wise to keep your changes far below that, for they can introduce errors in the final stages. Do your editing in manuscript; in the proof stages, make vital changes only.

Later on, when the pages of the book have been all made up into forms to be put on the printing press, your project manager and printer will be checking *blueprints*, also called *bluelines* or simply *blues*, which are copies of your composed pages. Blueprints can also be called *brownprints*, *silver prints*, *vandykes*, and by several other names, depending upon the process used. For author-publisher purposes, you need only know that they all perform the same basic function. They will also draw *press proofs* in order to take a final look at the book just before printing. If yours is an illustrated book, you too will want to look at copies of these final press proofs.

Paper Selection

Like any other publisher, you should seek a paper that most economically suits the content of the book and your aims. A paper suitable for an inexpensive newspaper that is destined to be thrown away shortly after purchase is entirely unsuitable for a book that is meant to last for decades. A paper quite suitable for a book composed entirely of print on paper may be quite unsuitable for a book composed largely of illustrations. A glossy paper that is wonderful for a highly illustrated book may be wholly inappropriate for an all-text work for the very reasons that make it good for illustration reproductions; the bounceback of light from a hard, very white, glossy paper may be fine for light, airy copy, but almost impossible for protracted reading of solid text.

Using other books as models may help you little in assessing suitability and price, for the book you choose from the library shelf may be made of paper far better and more expensive than anything you can reasonably buy today. Hidden inflation is the worsening of materials and the quality of work; it applies throughout the society, and to paper as much as anything else. Like commercial publishers, the self-publishing author needs expert buying help in this area. Publishers don't buy paper; their production departments do. Publishers make buying choices within the range of possible papers suggested by skilled production people. Self-publishers should try to work similarly, often buying paper with the help of designers and printers. As a practical matter, you are far more likely to buy your paper through a printer than to buy it yourself and ship it to a printer. You should strongly consider having the printer send you samples of papers that are readily available at the plant, which will generally be less expensive and more convenient than papers that must be specially ordered. What you very much need, however, is to know your book well enough to understand what qualities the paper should have to best suit the book.

There are a few basic characteristics you will want any book paper to have. First, a book paper must be opaque enough to be printed on both sides without any appreciable amount of "show-through," which is print from one side of the sheet showing as lines or shadows on the other side, making it hard to read.

Second, a book paper must be white enough to provide adequate contrast with the black type laid upon it, unless the paper is purposely made of some other color than white. To use a very inexpensive, low quality, grayish or brownish paper for your book is destructively penny-wise. It can destroy the entire appearance of your book and negate all your work and investment.

Third, a book paper should be capable of carrying adequately sharp and attractive reproductions of any illustrations you use. That does not mean printing a book with a few illustrations on expensive and inappropriate glossy stock. It does mean using a paper white enough and opaque enough to do decently by your illustrations—or reconsidering how and where you will use them. It is usually attractive to an author to carry illustrations in place within the book, where they will, if well-captioned, be most useful. Yet the tendency and desire to carry illustrations this way must be balanced against both the cost of paper and the risk of using the wrong paper for the text, which is probably the overwhelming bulk of the book. Sometimes it is far better to run your illustrations in a single group of pages, as so many other publishers do, and for similar reasons. Then you can use two papers, one for text and one for illustrations, with both right for the images they carry.

Fourth, the book paper you use should bulk properly for the size of book you want to publish. Type sizes, page margins, and trim sizes can control the number of pages in your book; paper bulk controls its thickness. A 256-page book on excellent but rather thin paper can look no thicker than a 100-page pamphlet, diminishing its value in the eyes of a potential buyer. The same 256-page book, on bulky, slightly more porous, but still highly readable paper, may be twice as thick and be recognizable as a book of an entirely acceptable and buyable size. Commercial publishers know and act upon this kind of understanding every day; so should self-publishers.

In book papers, the question of bulk has little or nothing to do with cost or weight. A bulky paper is not necessarily more expensive or more costly than a thin one. Actually, it is very often the reverse; some of the most expensive book papers used are very thin, dense, opaque "bible" stocks, suitable for use in very large, long-lasting reference books.

How long the paper in a book will last is a matter of deep concern for most book publishers. An extraordinarily large number of the books now in libraries and bookstores will literally self-destruct in the next couple of decades because of the high sulfuric acid content of the papers used in them. That is a worldwide phenomenon. How the use of self-destructing paper in books came to be generally accepted in publishing is something for future generations to study and deplore. In this generation, though, some alternatives are now available.

It is possible for any competent book production person or printer to order and use acid-free or largely acid-free paper in your book if you want your book to last. It is usually (but not always) somewhat more expensive than most equivalent self-destructing acidic book papers, but those cost relationships are changing as publishers seek acid-free paper for more of their books. When the time comes for you to produce your book, be sure to compare the prices of acid-free and self-destructing paper, so that you can make an informed decision as to which way to go. Should you have any difficulty in finding proper comparisons, calls to a few of the paper merchants and paper mills listed in *Literary Market Place* (see Appendix 1, Sources of Information) will allow you to find the information you want quickly and easily.

Pricing and Printing

It is at this stage that you bring into play the questions of pricing and printing discussed in Chapter 4, taking into account your estimated production costs, anticipated marketing costs and modes, likely revenue per book from the expected mix of sales, and the range of prices for similar books in the marketplace.

In deciding on the size of your printing, you may wish to keep in mind the rule of thumb by which many commercial houses operate: print at most the number of books you expect to be able to sell in the first year, and no more. Book storage often costs money, remember, and books held for long periods are subject to some of the same problems as unbound sheets held in storage. You can always print more as needed. Indeed, if prepublication response is extremely favorable, you can even go back to press again before actual publication; be very careful of this, however, for good reviews do not always translate into hard sales, and large returns may result from large advance orders. You may sink a great deal of money into an extra printing that you will not recoup so easily.

The price itself should be set early enough to be included on your various prepublication promotion pieces. Note that if production problems cause your costs to be much higher than expected, you can change the price on publication, if necessary. Try to avoid that, however, for it causes a great deal of confusion and extra handling in order processing.

The Body of the Book

Going from composed, corrected, laid-out pages to a finished book is done in several steps, which together are the balance of the publishing process. Reviewing those steps can help identify some of the key choices to be made.

Once the pages have been completed, they are made up into *forms*, which are groups of composed pages ready to be placed upon a press and printed. For offset printing, which is the standard mode of printing used in book publishing today, the form is an offset printing plate developed photographically. The older kind of form is the metal printing plate, which is still in very limited use for some kinds of periodical and special-purpose printing. For many years, the normal size of the form used in book production has been sixteen or thirty-two pages; that is why printers and publishers often speak of book lengths in multiples of these numbers, such as 224, 256, 288, or 320 pages.

Forms placed on presses are then *run*, or printed, with the number of books or other publications produced called the *press run*. It takes printers time to properly place each form upon the press after removing the previous plate—often more time than it takes to print a relatively short run of that form on a fast press. That is the main reason why short runs cost so much more per unit than longer runs do. More recent printing technology uses a film-to-print system that largely does away with plates and the extra expense they involve. As a result, much shorter runs have become far more economical.

A printer's available equipment can greatly affect the cost of a printing job. Aside from know-how, the main reason for using an experienced short-run book printer to produce your book is that such a printer is likely to have the right equipment to do the job economically and well. Another printer, however skilled, may not have quite the right equipment. For example, a printer whose press is not quite the right size for your requirements may waste a good deal of paper. A printer with a wonderfully fast press may be superb for long press runs, but inappropriate for your book because changing plates on that press takes so long. A printer can be undertooled, overtooled, or just not quite properly tooled to competitively meet your needs.

Even among experienced short-run book printers it is desirable to get competitive quotes. That is particularly so when those printers are bidding on a whole job, which involves their supply or purchase of composition, bindings, and paper. Those competitive bids must be in writing, and itemized; to have only a verbal and unitemized quote is like having no real quote at all.

On the following page is an illuminating set of project management and book manufacturing estimates, prepared by Robert Pigeon of Combined Publishing. These are for the book described in Table 1—5,000 copies of a 256-page 6" × 9" hardcover, composed mostly of text, with 20 illustrations of various kinds and averaging a little over 400 words per printed page.

Using that sample estimate, total pre-manufacturing and manufacturing costs for 5,000 books would be $15,256–$16,576, or $3.05–$3.32 per book. Total for running 2,000 books becomes $13,041–$14,361, or $6.52–$7.18 per book.

The complexities and hard costs of publishing project management and manufacturing make clear the advisability of seeking professional help on the book production side.

The author-publisher really has little hands-on work to do at the printing and binding stage, aside from looking at blueprints, if necessary. At this point, you are—more than anything else—a buyer, and you need to be an extremely careful one, with or without the help of your own skilled project manager. Turning your work from a manuscript into a printed and bound book is probably the major speculative investment you will make as a self-publisher, unless you decide to go for broke—which some literally do—in promoting your book.

Table 2: Sample of project management and book manufacturing estimates for a 256-page 6" × 9" hardcover, with 20 illustrations, as described in Table 1 (pp. 94–95).

Premanufacturing production costs:
Project management fee: $600–$1,200
Convert standard word-processing files containing approximately 100,000 words, design for book elements, format for page layout, insert 20 images in text with captions, output 2 sets each of first-pass, second-pass, and final-pass page proofs: $4.00–$6.00 per page depending on layout and format complexity (256 pages: $1,016–$1,536). (Of course, self-publishers may submit camera-ready pages, appropriate applications files for film output, or Postscript files ready for film output.)
Design jacket/cover using 1 color image and prepare final application software for film output: $300–$500
TOTAL PRE-MANUFACTURING COSTS: $1,916–$3,236.
Manufacturing specifications: 6" × 9" trim, 256 pages, 55# white offset stock printing on narrow web, 2,000/additional Ms to 5,000, hardbound (.085 pasted oak boards, 3-piece case with spine cloth at 1.5" turnaround and side panel material, head and foot bands, burst notch binding) or paperback edition (perfect adhesive binding), jackets (4-color process on 80# C/1/S stock with film lamination) or covers (4-color process on 10 point C/1/S stock with film lamination)

Manufacturing costs:

	2,000 books	3,000 addl. books	5,000 books
Prep:	$1,500		$1,500
Blues:	175		175
Paper stock:	1,500	$650	2,150
Print and fold:	1,100	215	1,315
Hardbound bind:	2,300	800	3,100
Paperback bind:	750	200	950
Jackets:	1,950	180	2,130
Covers:	1,850	170	2,020
TOTAL	$8,535	$10,370	$13,340

Sample estimate prepared by Robert Pigeon, Combined Publishing, 476 West Elm Street, P.O. Box 307, Conshohocken, PA 19428; 610–828–2595; fax: 610–828–2603; e-mail address: combined@dca.net or rpigeon@dca.net

A few matters are worth further discussion at this point, largely to provide you with some language and concepts that will help you to communicate well with publishing professionals.

Printed sheets coming off the press are *folded* and *trimmed*, sometimes as part of the operation of a sophisticated press or total production process operation, and sometimes by separate bindery machinery, which is the older production style. The resulting groups of pages are called *signatures*. In hardcovered books, signatures keep their identity as such; they are normally sewn together, with their inner ends uncut. They lose their identity as signatures when trimmed on all four sides, as for insertion into flat-backed, *perfect bound*, soft-covered books, or for insertion as drilled pages into looseleaf binders.

Sometimes for reasons of economy, a portion of the printed sheets coming off a press are not folded, trimmed, and taken on into finished books. Instead they are held as sheets and made up into books in small groups, after the initial body of books made has been sold out. Many vanity presses do that, to meet their contractual commitment to produce a certain number of "books"; they do not really expect ever to make the held sheets into books. Some publishers and self-publishers also hold sheets.

For some quite large books this can be a reasonably good way to economize. The hazard is that sheets held in storage are subject to spoilage. Printed sheets held at a printer's, or for that matter in your own storage facility, can spoil rather easily, and you may find that many of the sheets you have been storing at some expense for several years are not really usable when you want them. All it takes is a little mildew to spoil a whole bin-full or skid-load of printed paper. Likewise, a hot summer and inadequate ventilation can dry the paper out so much that it flakes and cracks, making it unusable. A slightly leaking outside wall, impregnation with an unwanted odor, or any of several other small disasters can befall stored paper.

Given today's short-run technology, it is, on balance, probably better to go ahead and manufacture all the books you think you should for your first printing and do subsequent printings as necessary. It is now possible to go back on press, even with a longish book, for as few as fifty to one hundred copies and still be able to sell fairly expensive books at a modest profit. Many printers advertise their short-run capability in *Small Press* and *Literary Market Place* (see Appendix 1, Sources of Information). If you are filling library orders and bookstores reorders, for example, even a book costing you $5 to remanufacture in smallish quantities can be sold profitably if its price is $19.95 or more and you charge for shipping or handling.

The folded and trimmed printed sheets are then gathered in proper sequence and made up into sets of book contents. How they are then handled depends on the desired binding. If they are to be put into a standard hardcover book, the signatures will most likely be sewn together by the *Smythe sewing* method. This uses a continuous thread, sews all the sheets in each signature together, and joins all the signatures with thread. The sewn signatures will then be glued to a strong flexible *backing*, using any of several modern adhesives. Then the now-sewn-and-glued contents of the book will be *cased in*—that is, pressed and glued into a *binding*, with glued *endpapers* providing the joinder between the book's contents and the inner covers of the binding. The binding will, in most instances, be made of some kind of plastic glued over binder's boards, generally called *boards*, which supply the hardness in the covers. It is also possible to do precisely the same kind of book with flexible covers, meaning essentially without boards.

If the book is to be softcovered, rather than hardcovered, and is quite slim, it can be covered in an inexpensive coated or uncoated paperback cover stock and *saddle-stitched*. That means it is bound together by only two or three staples, called *stitches*, set in vertically down the fold of cover and contents.

When the book is to be softcovered, but is thick enough to need a squared-off back, then it is *perfect bound.* This involves trimming all four sides of the folded signatures and relying upon adhesive to hold the contents of the book together and within the cover wrapped around it.

If the book is to be otherwise bound, all four sides of the signatures are trimmed. The resulting leaves of paper are then generally drilled and made ready for insertion into *comb, wire,* or *looseleaf binders,* in which metal or plastic is passed through the pages of the book, joining them together and holding them into the binder. Comb or wire binding devices are inexpensive and can make it possible to insert whole new sets of contents into the same binder periodically, as with yearly diaries. Looseleaf binders using posts or rings make it possible to insert pages in place in a book and are normally used in several kinds of topical reporting services. Rarely, a press binder is used, which holds undrilled pages solely by the pressure of the spring in the spine of the binder; this is an older and not very satisfactory binding method that is now little used.

How you make your book will depend upon your answers to several contingent questions relating to marketing, cost, content, and personal inclination. The author who has done a small book of poetry and intends to sell it mainly as an adjunct to live poetry readings may be quite correct to create a slim, softcovered pamphlet of a book, its heavy paper cover imprinted only with name of book and author, and saddle-stitched. That is by far the least expensive way to do such a book and will in no way hurt intended sales efforts.

On the other end of the spectrum, an author may intend to use a self-published book as basic outline and course material for an expensive business or financial seminar costing its participants or their corporate employers hundreds of dollars for a few days of discussion. That author is well advised to produce the contents of the book as cut sheets, drill them for insertion into an 8½" × 11" or 9" × 12" binder, and insert them into an expensive-looking, padded, gold-stamped looseleaf binder, complete with many blank sheets for notetaking. The little book of poetry may cost 50 cents to produce in small quantity, while the ring binder may cost $10 in similarly small quantity, a difference of $9.50 per unit. That seems quite a large difference—but the poetry book may sell for $7.95, and the ring binder may contain the only substantial piece of printed material in a course costing $795, a hundred times as much.

Most self-publishing authors will be seeking less special audiences than those sought by the poet and seminar author above. Rather than relying upon personal and seminar sales, they are likely to want to move books to market at least partly through bookstores and other bookselling outlets. Conventionally hardbound or perfect-bound softcover books will be most appropriate, selling side by side with tens of thousands of other such books, competing hard for shelf space and bookbuying attention. Most self-publishing authors will therefore have another modest but very significant production cost: the jacket of the hardcover or the cover of the paperback.

Jackets and Covers

A good book jacket or paperback cover does not merely *announce*; it *sells*. Personally or by mail, you can surround your book with all kinds of effective selling talk and technique, but in a bookstore you have just a few seconds to sell a potential purchaser. That is usually so even when someone has heard of your book through publicity or word of mouth. A few people come into a store entirely ready to buy, but not many.

Many book jackets and covers do not even announce well, much less sell effectively. A jacket placed spine outward on a shelf, as most books are, had best have its title large enough to be seen from across the store or from a lower shelf; otherwise it may very well be passed over, no matter how good, needed, and wanted it might otherwise be. A title printed in very artistic black on a dark red background may or may not win design awards, but will surely be unreadable from the normal distance between an aisle-browsing bookbuyer and a shelved book. It therefore might as well not be in the store for all the sales action it is likely to get.

Many books that do announce adequately still do not sell well. A title may give a potential buyer some sense of what the book is about, but subtitles and excellent selling copy on front and back covers are what it may take to draw that bookbuyer into a real consideration of the book. It may be commendably modest for the self-publishing author to refrain from self-glorification on the back cover of a paperback or the inside cover flap copy of a book—but many people want to think the book they are buying has been written by someone notable.

Economize everywhere else you can, but do not economize on

covers if you want to sell books in bookstores and other outlets. Hire an artist who has done excellent covers for others to do one for you. You can find the right cover artist/designer in *Literary Market Place* or through other publishing professionals.

You may also hire a copywriter to write the copy for your covers, but that is not as crucial as getting the right artist. For many books, whether published by others or self-published, it is the author alone who knows enough about the work to effectively put the words on paper that will sell it. It may be very hard to find a good copywriter to do the cover copy for your book, and unnecessarily expensive, though you would be wise to have an experienced copy editor go over your work before it is printed. On the other hand, those relatively few self-publishers who have decided to make a substantial investment in promotion may very well want to include cover copy and the securing of cover art in the arrangements they make with hired promotion and publicity people. Covers will prove extremely important in your selling efforts, especially for bookstore sales. Now then, we can turn directly to the matter of taking your finished book to market.

Paperless Publishing

Computers have brought with them new forms of publishing. It is now possible to publish works of all kinds, new or old, in forms that do not involve paper at all. Books can appear on floppy disks or on CD-ROMs. They can also appear in no material form at all, but as words and images transmitted through cyberspace over the Internet or various online services. This is still a relatively new area of publishing, including self-publishing, and it remains to be seen how it will develop. New forms and patterns will undoubtedly emerge as time goes on.

As with other kinds of publishing, the editing, design, composition, and production functions are best done by professionals working under your direction. You will find some of them in *Literary Market Place* and BookWire (see Appendix 1, Sources of Information); others will advertise in publications aimed at independent and nontraditional publishers or online at various book-related sites. They are not as numerous as print-on-paper publishers, so you may have to search a little. But be sure you are working with people who have experience specifically in publishing via electronic forms, which calls for considerable computer expertise and also for different kinds of design and handling functions than traditional publishing does. Computer users may want to look at the website of Impressions Book and Journal Services (www.impressions.com), which includes a discussion of electronic publishing, including some technical considerations in this fast-changing field.

The main problem with paperless publishing is not on the editorial and production sides, but in marketing, for people have not—or at least not yet—formed the habit of buying books in electronic forms. Print-on-paper books have been with us for centuries and people are used to reading in this form. Books have some enormous advantages. They are lightweight and portable; you can read them under an apple tree or in a bubble bath. You can easily flip back and forth to reread a section, and can pepper a book with flags marking passages of interest. The black-on-white print is easy to read. Books require no external energy source. Electronic books—roughly the size of traditional books—are being developed that may match some of these advantages of traditional books and also add others, such as searchability. The questions remain: How long will it take for technically sound, readable hand-held electronic books to be developed— and how long will it take bookbuyers to accept electronic books?

Another key question is: How long will it take for people to accept that they need to pay for material received electronically? Because enormous amounts of information are available for free over the Internet, many people have not been accustomed to paying for publications received online. The main exceptions have been areas of special interest, such as technical or academic publications that are made available to subscribers only. Some self-publishers have tried making their books available chapter by chapter, on a subscription basis, but such approaches are still very new and their long-term usefulness and commercial viability remain unclear.

At its most basic, however, publishing in electronic form can offer an author with limited resources a way to bring a work to readers without the expense of producing a print-on-paper book. Authors who publish their own works online, or in any electronic form, should be especially careful to register their copyright in a timely way, however, since electronic versions of a work can easily be copied and claimed by others. Piracy is an increasing problem in publishing altogether, but especially in electronic publishing.

Meanwhile, electronic routes offer some new and exciting ways of selling traditional books, which we will discuss more fully in Chapter 6.

CHAPTER 6

·····························

Selling and Fulfillment

The selling process starts long before your finished book comes off the press. In the widest sense, it starts while you are writing the book, as you speak with local advertising, newspaper, and broadcast people who may help you promote it, to local booksellers who may sell it to their customers, and even to individuals who may buy the book.

In a more practical and operational sense, the selling process starts when you begin to make the prepublication moves that will, together, provide the framework within which the book will be sold. Some of them are the prepublication editorial steps previously discussed. The Library of Congress Cataloging in Publication (CIP) and Advanced Book Information (ABI) registrations fall into this category, for example, as both bring your book to the attention of library and other bookbuyers, and make it easier to buy.

Throughout this chapter, we will be discussing selling moves, all or almost all of them costing something, either in out-of-pocket cash or in time. Most self-publishing authors will do some basic promoting and selling, but few will have the time or money to engage in large-scale promotion and selling. How much you do in these areas is entirely optional, beyond a few basic moves that it would be wasteful to omit. For almost every book, some sales are out there just for the informing and asking.

No matter how low your selling budget or how limited your selling time, you should take at least the basic steps to tell others that your book is for sale and to make it easy for people to buy it, by placing it before them. At the very least, those who are geographically or professionally close to you should have a chance to buy your book. That means, at a minimum, placing your book in book outlets, at least locally and probably regionally, and placing professional books before colleagues, at least by national advertising in professional publications and probably by nationally distributed mail-order efforts directed toward that narrow market.

Beyond those kinds of minimum efforts, only available time, money, and dedication impose limits. You can do a little; you can also publish a book, spend all your spare time and then all your time selling it, carry it around the country as the basis of a road-show lecture series, and turn it—quite literally—into a career. Some have; some bestsellers and careers have been born that way, by people publishing their own books and publishing through others.

Selling Is Selling

In a very real sense, selling is selling, whether you are selling books or furniture, whether you are self-publisher or small manufacturer, selling directly both to consumers and to the trade.

With your publisher's hat on, it is important to bear that in mind. With books in hand, you become both author and small business owner, selling your books to consumers directly and to those who resell them to consumers. Some self-publishing authors will not sell to the trade at all. An academic, for example, may sell an expensive book only through professional publications and to colleagues directly by mail. Conversely, some will sell only to the trade for resale. Attempting to sell your first novel directly by mail would probably be a waste of promotion money.

There is an unusual wrinkle to bear in mind when selling books: your sales to the "trade" for resale are not really sales at all, for the overwhelming majority of "sales" by publishers to booksellers in the

United States carry full return privileges. If you sell ten copies of your book to a bookstore, you may get them all back as "returns" and be obliged to issue a refund to the bookstore for the full price originally paid you. Yet, you must still push hard to make that "sale" to the trade, for your book is competing for floor space in stores that cannot possibly hold more than a small fraction of the hundreds of thousands of books in print in the United States alone, with tens of thousands more being published every year.

For many kinds of books, you have at least regional, probably national, and possibly international audiences to reach and sell, an embarrassingly large number of possible sales moves, limited time, and usually very limited resources with which to work. You need to sharply identify those who might most logically be expected to buy your book, and spend your available time and money to reach them. That means selling hardest and most effectively to those booksellers who are most likely to be able to sell your book to its logical audiences, and selling directly, when that is warranted, to your best lists of prospective bookbuyers.

A scattershot approach to selling your book is pointless and wasteful. If your book will appeal to, at most, 1,000 specialist libraries and 4,000 professionals in your own field, by all means sell it by mail and by concentrated professional journal advertising. Use a library jobber to reach those special libraries, relying for help on the recommendations of your colleagues and reviews in specialist publications. A broadcast press release and a strong effort to place the book in general bookstores will not help much. And if you do manage to place that kind of book in general bookstores, rather than in the few specialist bookstores that will sell it effectively, you will probably only get the books returned later on. In essence, they will have been stored for a little while in the bookstores, rather than in your own home, office, barn, or warehouse.

On the other hand, a popular book may sell modestly in general bookstores, develop momentum, and then profitably soak up as much time as you have to put into it, itself generating the cash you need to promote it widely. All depends on the book you have created and the audiences to which it is directed.

There are several important selling things to do while your book is in production and before it is in your hands. This period is when most well-established publishers engage in the bulk of their sales and marketing activities. You may not be able to do nearly as much as they can without your book to actually show, but you can do a good deal in this period to help sell your forthcoming book.

Advance Copies and Prepublication Reviews

In addition to the Library of Congress Cataloging in Publication (CIP), International Standard Book Number (ISBN), and Advance Book Information (ABI) registrations discussed earlier, one of the most useful prepublication activities is sending advance copies of your composed manuscript to those several key publications that generally review books only before they have been published. These advance manuscript copies are uncorrected page proofs of your book, usually without illustrations and final corrections, and with a plain glued-on paper cover carrying only the name of book and author. These bound proofs are sometimes still called bound galleys, though galleys—long single columns of type, not set into pages—are now uncommon, given modern computer composition. Any experienced book printer will be able to supply bound proofs. This is a very desirable thing to do at this stage of the publishing process, and especially for self-publishing authors, who can benefit greatly from favorable reviews in key publications and lose little from unfavorable ones.

Sending out prepublication copies will by no means guarantee favorable reviews—or any reviews at all, for that matter. No publication reviews more than a small fraction of all the books published in the United States each year. But you cannot get a hit unless you step up to bat. The right favorable review of your self-published book can mean the sale of enough copies to get your investment back, and perhaps then some.

You will also want to send advance copies to *Publishers Weekly*. Note that this periodical will very seldom review books after publication, as it is directed primarily to the book trade, which orders for resale in book outlets before publication. Most booksellers pay considerable attention to *Publishers Weekly* reviews, and a favorable review can mean some hundreds or thousands of prepublication stock orders from booksellers. They will still have to sell your book, and you may get many of them back—as booksellers will be "buying" from you with full privileges to return books for full credit—but you may get national distribution started from a single very favorable *Publishers Weekly* review.

You will also want to send advance copies to *Library Journal* and *Booklist*, both covering the vitally important library markets. Many thousands of libraries throughout North America buy directly from favorable reviews in these publications. A "highly recommended" in *Library Journal* can mean 2,000–4,000 direct sales of your book to libraries of all kinds. These publications will review postpublication, but your best bet is to send advance copies. For self-publishing authors, the importance of favorable reviews in these publications cannot be overstressed. Such reviews can mean relatively painless national distribution of your book to libraries, and the recouping of all your out-of-pocket costs—sometimes much more.

You may also find it useful to send advance copies to the *New York Times Book Review*, for the relatively small chance that your book will be reviewed in that highly selective publication, and to *Kirkus Reviews*.

When you do send advance copies, send a letter along with them, addressed by name to the publication's book review editor. Current names and addresses are carried in *Literary Market Place*. Don't be afraid to "sell" yourself and your book in your letter. Professionalism has little to do with "coolness." Tell the editor who you are, how you brought special qualifications and powerful motives to bear in writing the book, and why you are proud of the book that resulted. Be sure to include biographical material, expected publication date, and retail price, and, if possible, the ISBN number and Library of Congress Cataloging-in-Publication Data about your book.

Send bound proofs at least sixty days before your announced "publication date," and no more than ninety days before that date. Allowing less time than that may hurt your review chances, for books must be sent out by editors and reviews received back in time for publication. But announcing a later date may also hurt your chances, for busy editors may push your book to the bottom of a more timely pile of work and forget that it is there.

Bear in mind that your announced publication date is little more than an estimate you are making as to when finished books will have moved from printer to you and then out into the hands of booksellers. It is *not* when you receive finished books, for you must take into account the four to eight weeks it will take your books to reach any booksellers who have placed prepublication orders. It is safest to let your receipt of final proofs from your printer trigger setting a publication date ninety days later—as long as your printer assures you that the book is going right into whatever bindery operations will be needed to produce the book. If you have any real doubt on that, hold the advance copies until you are sure of actual production schedules and can then send them ninety days before your expected publication date.

Getting Usable Recommendations

Sales of your book can be enhanced by getting early recommendations from other people to use on jackets and covers, and in other advertising and promotion pieces. It will not help much to have your next-door neighbor fulsomely praise your novel on the back of its jacket; but it can help your nonfiction work to carry a recommendation by a well-recognized name in its field. And it can help even more to have a well-known and respected name attached to a preface or introduction to your book, with that name under yours on jacket or cover, and on the title page.

Getting a useful preface or introduction will require previous close acquaintance with the right kind of person or a good introduction from a mutual friend. That can be a matter of reaching out to former teachers, current colleagues, or family and friends; it will seldom be achieved cold. Someone who may write an introduction will always want to study an advance copy of your completed manuscript, long enough before it goes into production, for the introduction itself must be written and edited. Writing such a piece for a self-publishing author is a very considerable favor—even if a token payment from the author or a modest share of the author's revenues from book sales is part of the arrangement, as is often the case. It can also be rather a bother for the self-publishing author, for a slow introduction writer may badly bend anticipated production schedules and publishing arrangements, and a hypercritical one may spend a great deal of wasteful time going back and forth with the author on trivial questions. Still, there can be great value in such a preface or introduction for some kinds of books, especially those appealing to narrow markets, when the author is a relative unknown. It can be very worthwhile to get a preface or introduction that praises and recommends your work from someone who can influence others to buy your book.

Less important, but still quite useful, is the recommendation secured early enough to be used on the jacket (for a hardbound book) or cover (for a paperback) and early promotion pieces. Later, you hope to be able to join these kinds of recommendations (called *blurbs*) with favorable reviews. Some such early recommendations may be available for the asking after little more than a cursory examination—if that—of a few chapters of completed manuscript or of advance copies. A friend or colleague may very well do that for you, essentially asking you what to say. Others—and this will more often be the case—will take a much longer and harder look before publicly recommending your work. These people should be sent advance copies right off the press to give them time to read and recommend, if they will.

Here, too, you are likely to already know or be personally introduced to those whose recommendations you solicit. But it does not hurt at all to send advance copies to a few carefully selected people whom you do not personally know, but whose recommendations you would prize, if you think their interests and yours coincide and that they might indeed favorably comment and be willing to be quoted. In that case, be sure to send a rather full personal letter with the advance copies, telling them why you admire them and their work, why you are sending them the copies, how much their comments would be appreciated, and hoping that they would be willing to be quoted.

Early Promotion Efforts

Before your finished book is in hand, there are some very basic promotional preparations to be made. These involve making a list of those to whom you will be sending a press release announcing publication of your book; the writing of that press release; making a list of reviewers to whom you will be sending review copies of your finished book; the creation—but not yet placement—of any advertisements you will be running to coincide with publication; the selection of advertising media; and, if you are planning direct mail sale of your book, selecting lists, writing copy, and creating the mail package.

In these areas, you must make some very basic decisions as to the possible use of professionals, decisions that will rest considerably upon how much you are planning to spend to promote your book. If you are planning to spend $500–$1,000, and more later if the work generates the cash to do so, your promotion efforts will be very much a do-it-yourself matter. But if you have $5,000–$10,000 to spend, you may profit greatly by spending some of it on the kind of effective help you can get from those who routinely advertise in *Literary Market Place*. You are quite likely then to get far more sales for your money than a do-it-yourself effort might yield. If you are planning to spend more than $10,000, by all means get some professional help. A single substantial ad in a national magazine may cost $15,000 or more, and be a total waste of money for your particular book, when a few thousand spent on ads in carefully selected special-interest publications may prove enormously lucrative. A professional can advise you on the best use of your money in these areas.

The kind of book you have done will also affect this decision. If you are a professional, writing a book in your own field, with small, well-defined audiences, you may very well be able to handle promotion yourself, perhaps with the help of a competent local freelance copywriter. Then it may not matter whether you plan to spend $500 or $10,000 to promote your work, as you probably know the publications, reviewers, libraries, and selling appeals better than anyone advertising in *Literary Market Place*—and you may indeed be planning to sell your book primarily off the lecture platform. But if you are writing a general interest book, and have what seems to you a substantial amount of money to spend on promotion, by all means get professional help. It is a big country, and your promotion money can vanish tracelessly if used unskillfully. A few big non-selling ads, an expensive mail campaign that does not work—and your money is gone, when it might have been used to announce well, stir buying interest, and develop a little selling momentum to generate cash for wider selling efforts.

Press Releases and Review Copies

The press release announces your book. It should be sent to all print and broadcast media you feel might conceivably announce publication of your work. It is wise to take the time to carefully compile the list of those whom you think should receive that release, also noting which of them print or broadcast book reviews. That list should include all such media in your local area and all special-interest media that cover the particular content of your book. For example, a book about guns should be announced to all local media and all the main gun-related periodicals as well. A work in engineering, aimed at professionals, should routinely be announced to local media, but more important should be announced to the publications of the profession. A novel or general nonfiction book should be announced locally and to a wide range of major print and broadcast media, including the wire services. *Literary Market Place* has an excellent selection of reviewing media that can be used for both press release and review purposes. The *Standard Periodical Directory*, which is found in most even modestly substantial libraries and also has a website (www.mediafinder.com), is an excellent source for special interest publications since it breaks down its many thousands of periodical entries by interest group and supplies the kind of basic information you need for compiling your list. (For more on these publications, see Appendix 1, Sources of Information.)

The press release itself is basically a brief newspaper article. Those who announce your work after receiving your release may simply take the top of your release and print it, so be very sure to create a letter-head that includes the name of your publishing company, an address, and a telephone number. (A good example of a press release is given in Appendix 5.) Then, at the top of the release, be sure to note that your book is new, having just been published or "released," and give the name of your book and its price. In the text of the release, be sure to tell very briefly, right in the first paragraph, what the book is about, and follow that up with what you believe will make it most attractive to those you consider the book's main audiences. Also include a brief biography of yourself, the author, in no more than a short paragraph or two. For local and main professional publications, include a 5" × 7" head-and-shoulders photograph. A printed release looks neat, but a typed and double-spaced release looks more immediate and like a let-ter that should be read. Bear in mind that the first page of your release may be read, sometimes attentively—but that the second page may only be scanned, and subsequent pages are quite likely to be ignored by busy media people who will not take the time to boil down effu-sive prose into a very brief print or broadcast announcement of your book. You should be able to say whatever you have to say about your book very well in two pages or less, adapting and probably shortening your own jacket or cover copy to do so. If you find that you can't ac-complish it in two pages or less, get someone who can.

Your list of potential reviewers will be somewhat shorter than your press release list, largely because many of those on your press release list do not carry book reviews. For the main national review media, *Literary Market Place* will be most helpful; for special-interest maga-zines, *The Standard Periodical Directory* is best. The local library will have copies of local periodicals with the names of reviewers listed. For local broadcast media, pick up the phone and ask the stations who handles book reviews; then send review copies to those people by name.

You may want to call both local periodicals and local stations di-rectly, possibly prepublication, if your book is likely either to be of general interest or to fit into programming aimed at special interests. Then you can begin early to reach for both reviewers and potential interviewers. For example, a local-origination cable channel may very well have a cooking program on which you can effectively plug your new cookbook, or a self-help program on which you can push your new work in popular psychology.

Advertising Plans

This prepublication period is also the best time to decide where any ads are to be placed, and to write those ads. You should not place them, however. Even though you will need lead time to meet publication and closing dates—that is, those dates after which ads will not be accepted for a particular publication—there is time enough to place ads once books are actually in your hands. If your promised book is delayed, or is perhaps unacceptable as received from your printer, you may be unable to pull any prematurely placed ads, wasting your precious resources.

For a general book, get some professional help to evaluate ad placements and to help write ads if you possibly can, even if that help is part-time, local, and not terribly experienced at advertising books. Even for a professional book aimed at narrow markets it may pay to get some professional help in this area. The special language of advertising alone may frustrate your efforts, even if you know exactly which ads to place where and think yourself able to write a reasonably good ad that will appeal to professional colleagues. Matters of circulation, size of ad, cost, placement, and frequency of insertion must also be considered, as well as the matter of creating an ad that sells. Most authors are entirely amateur in this area, not realizing, for example, that a too-small ad might better not have been placed at all.

Similarly, your advertisements should often include a coupon, which allows the reader to buy the book directly. An ad without a coupon may be all right for some general books readily available from bookstores, but is entirely wrong for a self-published book that might not have very good bookstore distribution. Many booksellers do not like ads that include coupons, reasoning that such ads detract from their business, so they often pressure commercial publishers not to sell books directly through ads with coupons. But coupons make it easy for prospective buyers to buy, so the self-publisher who does not include them is often largely wasting the money spent for the ad.

Selection of advertising media can be an easy affair when dealing with books directed to narrow markets and a very difficult affair when dealing with general books. If there are two main magazines in your specialized field, you may find that your scholarly or professional book is best advertised in them alone, perhaps rather prominently and repeatedly. You may also advertise in whichever library journal is best distributed in your field. A general interest book, on the other hand, may best be advertised to the trade in *Publishers Weekly*, to the library market in *Library Journal*, and to general readers hardly at all, as your limited promotion money may more fruitfully be spent in other ways. Certainly you may want to consider advertising in the *New York Times Book Review* if you have had a favorable review there—but it hardly pays to advertise your self-published book modestly in the back pages of that publication. For those rare self-publishers who can afford to advertise a financial or self-help book via full page ads in many newspapers around the country, the game is entirely different—but those are self-publishers working with hundreds of thousands of dollars in advertising budgets and a great deal of professional help.

Direct Mail Selling

Most self-publishing authors will properly want to do some direct mail solicitation of sales, if only to relatives, friends, coworkers, and colleagues. Do try hard to resist the natural inclination to proudly give away hundreds of copies of your work to such people. At rock bottom, their purchases may make the difference between getting your cash investment back and losing much of it—and therefore between doing only one self-published book or having the cash to self-publish others.

A mailing to such a personal-contact list should include: a letter, adapted from your jacket and cover copy and press release; a coupon selling the book at full price, which also provides for multiple purchases of the book, perhaps at a small discount; and, where appropriate, a personal note from you, either separately or handwritten on the letter. This is all very much worth the effort; people close to you will buy, and sometimes in multiples, for gifts and to supply to others interested in your work—people you may not even know. You will have been talking about the book for quite some time with many people, and their interest and curiosity may have been stimulated far more than you had realized. Openly solicit them to buy; they can mean a lot to you.

You may also wish to do basically the same kinds of mailings to certain kinds of lists of prime prospective purchasers, especially when your book is priced relatively high and likely to be bought by relatively small groups of purchasers. Otherwise, the economics of mail-order selling will conspire to defeat the self-publishing author of a single book.

Some extraordinary self-publishing successes have been achieved with direct mail. But mail selling can also be an expensive trap; it must be handled well, which means first of all handling it very carefully.

Mail-selling economics are simple enough to understand, but a surprising number of self-publishers do not take the trouble to understand them and thereby either lose a good deal of money or fail to take advantage of the main selling opportunities for their books. In mail selling, you have to get at least enough cash back out of the mailing to pay for the cash you put in; that includes the cash cost of the mailing itself, the book you supply to purchasers, and order fulfillment and billing. If you were a full-fledged commercial enterprise, you would also have to pay for the time you put into the mailing, the time you spend fulfilling and billing orders received, and certain overhead costs. You might also then be willing to offset some costs by figuring that sales through other outlets might be enhanced by the advertising value of your mailings, but that is a very unwise supposition for self-publishers with one book to sell.

The same comments, in numbers, come out something like this: Assume that you are selling a general interest book, and that a mailing sent out at bulk rates comes to 35 cents per piece, after you have figured in all the costs of renting an appropriate mailing list or lists, paper, envelopes, printing, postage, and professional help if any. (It probably will come out higher, especially when the mailings are as small as a few thousand pieces.) That comes to at least $350 per thousand pieces mailed. Further assume that you sell successfully to one percent of those mailed, that your book costs $20, and that total costs per book manufactured, shipped, and billed come to $5 each (a very rough approximation, but adequate for purposes of this discussion). You have sold one percent of 1,000 pieces mailed, or 10 books, for total revenue of $200, and have spent $350 for mailing and $50 more for books sold, for cash costs of $300. Your out-of-pocket cash loss showing is therefore $200 per thousand pieces mailed, and is probably even higher, as costs here are modestly stated, and no allowance has been made for collection problems. You have also spent a good deal of wholly uncompensated time.

But if your book is a high-priced, special-interest book, or a high-priced book that will be bought primarily by libraries, the numbers can change greatly. With a special interest book sold at $35, and allowing for the bigger book to cost $6 instead of $5 to fulfill, you show a net cash return, above costs, of $525 per thousand on mail solicitations. With a successful mailing like this, you can solicit the same list over and over again with the profits from the first, for a good mailing list keeps on buying, sometimes better on solicitations a few months later than on original solicitation. That means you will probably be able to solicit the list many times, ultimately getting many hundreds of very profitable sales from a highly responsive list, and with a very small initial cash outlay for mailings.

Should you decide to do mail solicitation on your own, do bear in mind that your coupon offer should make it possible for corporations, libraries, and other institutions to be billed by you, rather than having to attach a check or specified kind of credit card number with the order. These kinds of buyers will have to go through internal procedures to issue you a check, which will usually require a billing. But consumers—including your friends, family, and colleagues—should be required either to send a check with their orders or attach a credit card number, after you have made arrangements with a credit card company to honor such orders. Visa and MasterCard are probably best for this, being most widely used and charging you less for this service than some other credit card companies. If you want to make it a little easier for consumers to buy by mail for what is essentially cash, offer a full money-back guarantee within thirty days if they are not completely satisfied with their purchase of your book. As so many mail-selling organizations have found, the rate of return for refund on this kind of offer is usually negligible.

For anything much beyond personal-contact mailings and the kind of narrow-market mailings described above, it is wise to secure professional help. Like advertising, mail marketing can be a very dangerous trap for the unwary. Many important questions surround proper list selection and use, including how to go about finding the right lists; which lists are most likely to be live and responsive; how to go about testing lists, rather than throwing money away on mass mailings that may not work; how much to pay for list rental; how to handle bulk mailings; and a good deal more. Two lists that look quite the same to the amateur may be as different as night and day to the eye of the mail-order professional.

That will also be so for the creation of the mailing package. For example, a wrong choice of too-heavy paper may cost you a great deal in additional postal costs, while an unclear offer or coupon may cost you a good many sales. If you intend to engage in any substantial direct-mail marketing activities, you will be wise to secure professional help, either from *Literary Market Place* or through local recommendations, from other self-publishers or through the recommendations of local advertising and mail promotion people.

Finding the Right Distributors

Self-publishing authors generally find it quite difficult to reach agreement with potential distributors, or to get firm orders from chains, individual bookstores, and nonbookstore outlets until they have finished books to show. A good prepublication review in *Publishers Weekly* can go far toward curing all that, but such reviews are scarcely to be expected and planned for. If you are fortunate enough to get one, the picture changes; everything we discuss in the following pages should be moved up, with the review and press release, and perhaps advance copies of covers, taking the place of finished books to show.

Normally, the period before books are in hand is a period of preparation in which you identify potential distributors and sales outlets, make some tentative approaches, and set yourself to move into action. The *American Book Trade Directory* carries substantial lists of book wholesalers and jobbers. A smaller, more selective, and therefore probably more useful list is carried in *Literary Market Place*. The latter publication also carries an essential list of most of the main book distributors and sales representatives; others, advertising in such publications as *Small Press* and *Publishers Weekly*, identify themselves as organizations wanting to represent small presses.

If your book is suitable for bookstore distribution, you should explore the increasing numbers of national distributors (listed in *Literary Market Place*), which together represent thousands of small publishers. Some regional and special-interest distributors may be especially appropriate for your particular book. You may, for example, reason that you will more effectively sell your book to bookstores in your own region and to chain bookstores than will any distributor representative carrying a catalog containing the books of several hundred other small publishers. At the same time, you should recognize that most booksellers prefer to deal with distributors rather than directly with very small publishers, and that where you cannot sell to a store personally, a distributor may be able to sell far more effectively than your mailed flyer for your single book can.

If you can get distribution by others—and for many self-publishers that is a big "if"—then a combination of personal selling and distribution arrangements is probably the best way to go. On the other hand, if your selling time is severely limited, or you are for any reason unwilling or unable to go out and actively sell your book, then you will need a distributor for your home area and someone to try to sell the chains.

You will have to sell to bookstores at 40 percent off list price, whether through others or directly yourself. Chains will demand and get at least 50 percent off list price, as will jobbers—not just from you, but from major commercial publishers as well. Distributors will often get 15 percent or more beyond that. Some distributors will supply considerable promotional and fulfillment help, although some warehousing and other fulfillment help may be charged separately. It is essential to carefully explore a potential distributor's willingness to represent you and to make the necessary economic arrangements long before you have books in hand. If at all possible, make your arrangements early enough so that you can instruct your printer to send books to any distributors; otherwise, if they come to you, you will bear the extra cost of reshipment to distributors. Bear in mind throughout, though, that effective distribution may be hard to achieve, and that you may have to do much of it yourself, personally and by mail.

Library distribution works differently. You can sell directly to libraries, or you can use distributors, who will sell at 20 percent off list price and charge you a distributor's percentage besides. It is penny-wise to try to do it all yourself, if a distributor such as Ingram or Baker and Taylor will stock your books. Librarians routinely order from such jobbers and partly depend on information supplied by such jobbers when making buying decisions. Call library distributors early, learn what they will need to represent you best, explore if they will indeed stock your books, and use them.

Once books are in hand, preparation time is over. Then it is time to place those ads, send those review copies, send the early mailings, and go out and sell your book, personally and through orders, using all the promotional skills and techniques you can muster, and through all the outlets available.

Personal Selling

As we have seen, there are many good ways to sell your book. The surest way of all, though—and the method best calculated to earn back at least your modest cash investment—is to take your book in hand and sell it directly to others. No, it won't break you even on cash outlays, if you have put a great deal of production and promotion money into your book; then you must rely mainly on the results produced by the skills of others and the returns achieved from the media used—just as any other publisher does. And yes, it will take some of your time, and your time (as previously discussed) is a very real cost element in self-publishing, as in any other venture. But allowing for all that, there is no surer way to get at least your cash out so that you can live to self-publish another day if you wish.

Let us suppose, for example, that you have just self-published 2,000 copies of your book, and that so far you have invested $10,000 in cash. You have decided to make your book a trade paperback and have set a $20 price.

On those books you sell directly to others at full list price you will receive $20 each. On those you place directly in bookstores—more accurately, those sold to customers rather than returned to you unsold—you will receive 60 percent of $20, or $12 each. Therefore, you can get your direct cash outlay back by selling as few as 500 books directly to others or as few as 833 through bookstores. If you sell both ways—and you should do so, if at all possible—your cash breakeven point will be somewhere between 500 and 833 sales. For book outlet sales, there may be some smallish related costs, such as for mailing, automobile expenses, or possible uncollectible bills, so you should figure that you really will break even on cash outlay somewhere between 600 and 1,000 sales. That is not very many sales and is well within the ability of most self-publishing authors to manage.

But breaking even is not all that is possible when you go out and personally sell your self-published book very aggressively. Astute personal selling can also make your book very profitable and provide greatly needed marketing money on a "bootstrap" basis, as well as lunch money, dinner money, and money to live on while you are writing your next book.

Direct selling at full price can be especially lucrative, and never more so than when you are able to sell your book from a public platform. That is true whether you are a poet giving a reading from your work, a local historian detailing a Civil War battle, or a devoted quilter sharing the techniques and lore of the craft. The people in any audience you speak to have, by their presence, indicated their interest in your topic—and are a built-in, ready, and often eager market for your book.

That is particularly true of self-published books in your own professional area. If you travel the country or region to speak at professional meetings, or as a professional to lay audiences, you will be able to sell significant quantities of your self-published book month after month, year after year, far beyond cash breakeven needs and deep into profit. If you are a professional and don't yet do that kind of lecturing, then by all means let the decision to self-publish also be a decision to hit the lecture circuit. You can build your contacts and get your feet wet as a public speaker while you are writing and publishing your book, and be ready to go when your book comes off the press.

What kinds of professionals can do this successfully? Most kinds, really, unless they are unable to do so because of professional association or licensing strictures. The learning disabilities specialist who speaks to parent groups can do it. So can the psychologist, sex therapist, employment counselor, nutritionist, dietitian, physical therapist, marriage counselor, lawyer, tax accountant, and financial advisor, to name just a few of the kinds of professionals who can profit handsomely by combining public speaking and self-publishing.

Professional or not, all it takes is making very sure that you have your book in hand and that you sell it from the platform before, during, and after the meeting. Do not just mention it diffidently, by the way—sell it, really sell it.

Having your book in hand is a lot easier when you are self-publishing than when you are working with a commercial publisher. Most commercial publishers are simply not geared to ensure that your books will be there to meet you when you arrive at a speaking site, as thousands of disappointed authors have discovered over the years. No such problem exists with your own self-published book, though. You just ship ahead by air express, with instructions to hold for your arrival, or take the books with you in your luggage. Of the two methods, and especially with relatively light paperbacks, we much prefer taking the books with you. Then you need not worry about the hotel mislaying your books and can also avoid some rather expensive air express shipping charges.

Effective platform selling means mentioning your book often, reading passages from it, telling people that it is for sale at the back of the hall and what it costs, and that you will autograph any copies purchased after the meeting. People expect all that. You may do it all with a diffident and disarming grin—but by all means do it. At many all-day meetings, it is possible to set up an autographing session at a break point, perhaps before or after lunch, with press coverage arranged by the meeting's sponsors. Professional association and trade press coverage are particularly valuable here, for they pave the way for invitations to other meetings and future coverage.

One of the key things to bear in mind here is that by aggressively selling your work, autographing copies, and reaching for press coverage, you are also helping to build the meeting and its sponsors. Never lose sight of the fact that authors enhance meetings and that authors who are well-known bring referred status to meetings and their sponsors. No matter how "unnatural" it may feel to push yourself and your work, do it, for it helps everyone concerned, not only you.

At some large meetings, it may be worthwhile to hire an exhibition booth from which to sell your book, whether or not you speak at the meeting. You must weigh the costs carefully, though. At a national or large regional convention, such a booth may cost several hundred dollars, and if you have not spoken at the convention, renting a booth may not be cost-effective.

Traveling is not the only way to sell self-published books from the public platform. Authors in any of the large number of subject areas covered by continuing education courses can very profitably combine teaching and self-publishing. That, for example, is how some very good cookbooks and crafts books have been born. And if you can successfully move into a combination of continuing education courses, community cable television activities, and self-publishing, you may discover a very profitable combination of activities, indeed. You may supply your self-published books to the sponsors of continuing education courses at a discount off cover prices; they may, in turn, supply your book as course material. That is probably the best way to handle it, but if necessary, you can supply the book directly to those attending the course at cover price or a modest discount.

Selling Through Local Bookstores

Just as national review attention enhances your ability to find good distributors, sell to libraries, and do successful mail marketing, so do local and regional publicity and direct selling help your ability to make effective book outlet placements. But even without very much direct promotion and sales activity, it is possible to achieve quite good local and regional book outlet placement for your self-published book if you go out, visit the stores, and ask them to stock your book.

Many authors balk at doing that, feeling that asking bookstores to stock their books smacks too much of vulgar commercialism. Nonsense—if you have published a book, you want an audience; the odds are that you are just a little shy and need an act of will to overcome that shyness. The truth is that if you have self-published a lovely little book containing some of your poetry, for example, and want to get at least your cash out so that you can easily do another, you are going to have to sell a little. That means trying to set up some readings at which you will sell your work to those who come; it also means going to bookstores and asking them to stock your book.

As any good sales professional will tell you, selling a bookstore on the idea of stocking your own self-published book is hardly selling at all. It is the rare bookstore owner, indeed, who will not be willing to find a little room somewhere for a few copies of your work; people who run bookstores are seldom so doggedly commercially minded as all that. If they were, they probably would be in some other, far more lucrative line of business. And, after all, no money necessarily changes hands when a bookstore stocks your work; it is the nearest thing to a sale on consignment, except that legal matters relating to who owns the book while it is in the bookstore's hands work a little differently. If a bookstore returns your unsold book within an agreed-upon time, that return is for full credit, with the book costing the bookstore nothing but the price of shelf space for the time it stocked the book. Independent, local, and regional bookstores are probably the best places for you to try, at least at the start. Some chains do not stock self-published books, though some may bend a rule if you have established a favorable sales record.

You will find almost all American bookstores listed in the *American Book Trade Directory*. The American Booksellers Association also has a directory of its members. Their CIBON Bookstore Directory is also available on-line (www.bookweb.org). Pick out those within as large an area as you are willing to travel to, and go to them. Don't choose their busiest times, though; a bookstore owner or bookbuyer in a shopping area will probably not want to talk with you about your book on a busy Saturday afternoon.

Even though no money will change hands immediately, you still may have some convincing to do, however, for bookshelf space in a store is the subject of intense competition between publishers. What will win the day for you—and get you the placement you want—is that you are the book's author, and that the book obviously means a very great deal to you. Let that show; "coolness" does not place or sell books—commitment does. Beyond that, though, it is up to you to think through and then tell bookstore people why customers are likely to want to buy your books, for the bookstore owner who does not sell enough books is soon out of business.

For local bookstores—that is, those close enough to expect book purchases from your friends and neighbors—there should be no problem of placement. Most bookstores will routinely stock local authors, and many devote a shelf or two to their most recent books. That is not just a matter of courtesy to you, by the way; they can expect to sell your books to those who know you and will buy your book for that reason alone, if for no other. Indeed, some local bookstores will want autographed copies to sell, and will feature them as such; by all means supply signed copies when requested.

Some local bookstores will be amenable to your suggestion that they advertise your book locally and organize an autographing session at the store, perhaps with some refreshments—especially if you are willing to chip in on the refreshments. Do suggest just that, even sharing some portion of a modest advertising cost. In book trade jargon, that is *co-op (cooperative) advertising*. It is good publicity and can help start what may turn into a good local sale of your book. Remember that sales develop best by word of mouth, and that the way to get good sales in your home area is to get some publicity, some early sales, and then recommendations from one neighbor to another.

Bookstore people further away may take a little more convincing. They are not very likely to be convinced that your book will sell because you tell them that it is superbly written or that the subject matter is a "hot" topic. They hear that every day from publishers' salespeople, who also promise national publicity and substantial advertising expenditures. Many of them will stock your book anyway, as we have discussed, because you are coming to them as an author with book in hand, but it is also wise to be prepared to tell them about your promotion plans. If you are trying to organize readings, seminars, lectures, or classes—whatever is appropriate for your kind of book—tell them so. If you are trying for community cable TV exposure, describe your plans. If you are working on an author interview in a local or regional newspaper, say so. Make it clear that you are putting a great deal of time and attention into the promotion of your book; then their natural inclination to stock it will be reinforced enough for them to make the right decision.

Getting Wider Bookstore Distribution

It is possible to get a surprisingly wide distribution of your book through personal selling calls on individual bookstores in your local area and region. Indeed, if yours is a local or regional book, that may be your prime means of achieving bookstore distribution. You may even reach the chains as individual major bookstores; local chain managers may recommend you to home office regional buyers when home office central buying is required. And if you are traveling to any extent with your book in hand, as on a lecture circuit, personal selling calls on bookstores along the way are very much in order.

If yours is a book that calls for national distribution in bookstores, though, and you are a relative unknown—perhaps an author with a first book that you have decided to self-publish—wider distribution can become a difficult problem. As we have discussed, the overwhelming majority of booksellers do prefer to deal with established distributors and publishers. We do recommend that you begin exploration early and try hard to find and effectively use one or more national, regional, or special-interest distributors. But that may be hard to accomplish, at least until you and your book have some early marketing successes to show. A favorable review in *Publishers Weekly* or one of the other major prepublication review media is that kind of early success. It favorably disposes booksellers to stock your books, which is after all what distributors are concerned about.

A substantial sale to one of the major chains—Barnes and Noble and Borders are the biggest, and all are listed in the *American Book Trade Directory*—should even more surely bring distributor attention. That kind of sale is likely to be a two-step affair, the first sale being to a single chain bookstore or a regional buyer in the chain's home office and the second sale the national sale. It is only logical for the chain to want to see how the book of an unknown self-publisher is likely to do in the marketplace before making a major purchase, even though the "purchase" is only a conditional one, with full return privileges. Store space, especially in a major chain, is at a premium and is hotly pursued by all trade publishers, large and small.

It is also important for you to want to see how your book will do in the chains before undertaking the substantial gamble that accompanies acceptance of a major order. A chain with 7,000–8,000 stores, which wants to stock an average of eight books per store, will place an order for 5,600–6,400 books. You then have to quickly—and therefore probably rather expensively—manufacture those books and ship them to the chain, spending anywhere from a few thousand dollars for a smallish trade paperback to as much as $20,000–$25,000 for a substantial, rather expensive hardcover book. That is quite a gamble, considering the possibility that, although the chain may sell out its first big order and clamor for more, it is at least equally probable that sales will not go well, and may even go very badly. You may wind up selling only a few hundred books and being swamped with thousands of returns from the chains. It happens every season to some books. Large commercial publishers lick their wounds, sell some returns elsewhere, remainder some, and offset the loss with more profitable books. But a self-publishing author with only one book can be bankrupted by a single experience like this.

Sell to chains, by all means—to single chain units, and to regional and national home office buyers. With book in hand, call the home offices of the chains and ask by name for that buyer you think most appropriate for your kind of book or geographical area. Be prepared to be referred around a bit on the phone; organizations and people change, even between the time a directory is set in type and the time you use it. When you do have the right buyer, make an appointment to see that person, if you can afford the time and money to make the trip and if he or she will see you. If not, discuss the book and arrange to send it, along with a covering letter, any favorable reviews, and promotional material (such as your press release) that you have developed.

If you can, it is usually far more productive to make a personal sales call with your self-published book, carrying in that kind of supportive material. Buyers cannot help but be impressed by your commitment, and although it may prove fruitless, it is far more likely to result in at least the kind of trial regional placement that is really the best way to go for both you and the chain. If you do find a chain buyer who wants to "go for broke" with your book, be careful; do your best to remember that if it all goes wrong, it is you, rather than chain or buyer, who will be broke.

You may be able to reach as many as a couple of hundred bookstores personally if you devote a good deal of time to the project over some months. You may also be able to reach thousands of substantial chain bookstores. But beyond these, there are thousands of book outlets, spread across fifty states, that you can reach only through one or more distributors or through your own advertising and mail-order activities. If you do use a distributor, by the way, do not expect a distributor's sales representative to personally call on every bookseller to sell your book hard. Far from it; sales representatives will be selling the work of as many as several hundred authors by catalogue in all-too-short sales calls on the larger booksellers. Many smaller booksellers will be sold exclusively by mail catalogue. You will focus on only one book when you sell; that is one of the main reasons why you are so much more likely to be effective at personally selling your work than the most experienced sales representative in the world. The other is that the book is yours, and even the most skeptical book-sellers find authors with their own works in hand hard to resist, face-to-face.

You can reach these thousands of book outlets by mail, whatever your other distribution arrangements. You can send them descriptive material on your work, with an order form and with the kinds of supportive materials you would take in on a personal call: recommendations, favorable reviews, and a list of chain and other major bookstore buyers. R. R. Bowker rents bookstore lists suitable for these purposes, or test lists may be compiled right out of the *American Book Trade Directory*.

Before spending thousands of dollars on a major mailing to all American hardcover and trade paperback book outlets, you would be wise to test the likely response. Spend a few hundred dollars on mailings to test lists of bookstores to see just how worthwhile this kind of expenditure is likely to be for your book. No matter how favorable the reviews or strong the chain store placements, individual mail-solicited booksellers may still not place your book in significant quantities. Many are conditioned to working with distributors—or it may be as simple and unfortunate as their having already stocked several well-publicized books on the same subject from large commercial publishers in that season. Yours may be one too many. In mail-order work of any kind, it is essential to limit commitment and spending, until testing shows promising enough results. The occasional amateur gambler "makes it big" in mail order without adequate testing, but will always come up broke sooner or later, usually sooner.

Selling on the Internet

Self-publishers have a host of new selling opportunities through the Internet. Some of these require no special computer expertise, but simply take advantage of promotional possibilities available on the World Wide Web. These include different ways of reaching traditional bookbuyers, reaching people who have not traditionally bought books, and also reaching across national boundaries to book buyers abroad.

At its most basic, self-publishers will want to list their books with the main Internet bookstores, such as Amazon.com (www.amazon.com), Barnes & Noble (www.barnesandnoble.com), Borders (www.borders. com), Books.Com (www.books.com), Altbookstore.com (www. altbookstore.com), and the England-based Internet Book Shop or iBS (www.bookshop.co.uk). These and other such sites make it easy for authors and publishers to list their books. Some of them also offer special features to help sell your book. Most notably, Amazon.com allows you to include an image of the book's cover, copies of reviews, excerpts, a synopsis, author comments, jacket copy, and even author interviews, so you can talk about the book, and how and why you wrote it, as well as about your experience as a writer and publisher.

You should take advantage of any such opportunity offered to you by online booksellers. Be sure to include in the description all the elements of the book that might interest readers, because a major advantage of online booksellers is that they allow potential bookbuyers to search their databases. Whether your book is about making beer, the Battle of Gettysburg, threats to the rain forest, or women spies, make sure you include any key word that readers might use in searching for books on those topics, so yours will pop up in such a search.

Several online booksellers also offer special programs for authors and independent publishers, such as the Amazon.com Advantage, Barnes & Noble's Affiliate Network, and The iBS Partnership Program. Though specifics differ, these plans generally involve the online bookseller taking over some of the self-publisher's selling and fulfillment functions. With some, such as Amazon.com Advantage, independent publishers place a few copies of the book in the bookseller's inventory, so they can be shipped in a day or two, rather than the three to six weeks that might be involved in handling the book as a special order. As the bookseller's inventory drops due to sales, more copies are ordered. Some may carry a self-published book only if they have an exclusive, so check the details of any program you are considering.

Such programs offer the biggest advantages to independent publishers or authors with their own websites, which include links to these online booksellers. Again, specifics differ, but in some programs if a bookbuyer follows a link from your site to the online bookseller, then you get a certain percentage of the *total* sale made by the bookseller at that time. Say you have a website featuring your quilting book and you participate in one of the above programs. That means if a bookbuyer visits your quilting site, follows the link to the online bookseller, and then buys three books—which may or may not include your own book—you will earn a percentage of the total sale.

Your Own Website

The self-publishers best positioned to take advantage of the Internet are those with their own websites. Many people already have their own websites, and even young children are now being taught how to set up a home page, which is the first page to appear at a website's main address. But, as with book production functions, you will be best advised to call in professionals to help you set up a site. Developing a website takes an enormous amount of time and expertise, since it involves using a new language (such as HTML) to specify the size, color, and placement of every single comma, period, letter, and graphic on the page. Even if you were willing to devote the time to building a website, a professional Web designer will do it far better than you could as an amateur, helping you think through what you want and what you need. As with book designers, however, you should be careful not to get too "fancy" in your design. That can make the site less readable and slow down the loading process, and so may cause people to move on before they have seen what you have to offer.

If you are considering setting up a website, take a look at other book-related sites on the Web; thousands of them are listed as links at BookWire (www.bookwire.com); for more on this site, see Appendix 1, Sources of Information. Makes notes about what you think works and what doesn't. Think about what you want to include, such as cover art, description of the aims and intentions of the book, table of contents, excerpts, reviews, favorable comments, schedule of author's tour stops, and the like. You should have a good idea of what you want, so you can describe to a Web designer what you want for your own site. Contacting a Web designer prematurely can cost you a great deal of time and money.

The cost is not small, and you will have to assess whether the online sales potential of your book will justify those costs. You will need to pay approximately $100 to register your *domain name*, the unique name for your website, for two years, and $35 a year after that. This registration is important, since you are building your own "brand name." You register the name online with INTERNIC (rs. internic.net/). That site includes instructions for registering and also a list of previously taken domain names. You will also pay perhaps $50 a month for the Internet Service Provider (ISP), from which you effectively rent space. A good way to find a list of Internet Service Providers (ISPs) is by searching on the Internet at Yahoo (www.yahoo.com). Beyond that, you should expect to pay as much as $2,000 or more to a Web designer to develop the site, plus somewhat more in the first year or two, if sales warrant it, to modify the site and take advantage of what parts work best. As with the overall self-publishing decision, a special-interest book with a narrowly defined market is more likely to justify the cost of Web design than a novel. However, some novels include elements that can help you find potential bookbuyers, such as a novel about the Civil War or one set in biblical times.

If you do decide to set up a website, you can sell to bookbuyers directly online or have them call a toll-free number to place an order. Either way, you will probably want to have credit card arrangements and, for online sales, you will want to arrange for a secure server, which encodes information in transit through the Internet. Alternatively, you may decide to refer buyers to an online bookseller with which you have established a relationship (such as the ones mentioned above). Many people have had success with posting an excerpt from the book online, as a sample of the whole book being offered for sale. Some people have even tried offering their books chapter-by-chapter, with the reader paying for each chapter as it is published, on a serial basis, the way many nineteenth-century novels were published. However, it is too soon to say whether that approach will work, and if so, for what kinds of books.

A website alone does nothing. You have to find a way to get people to visit your site and read about—and possibly buy—your book. First of all, you should register your site with the main Internet directories and search engines. These include Yahoo (www.yahoo.com), Infoseek (www.infoseek.com), AltaVista (www.altavista.com), Lycos (www.lycos.com), Excite (www.excite.com), and HotBot (www. hotbot.com). Some of these (notably Yahoo) have human indexers, who categorize sites based on intelligent analysis of their contents, but most use computer-generated indexes to words in your site, so be sure your site contains all the key words and information, properly tagged, that would direct people to it.

Another way to get people to visit your site is to set up reciprocal links with other sites. Search out appropriate sites related to your book or topic; include links to such sites in your own site, and ask those sites to do the same for yours. And certainly request to list your site in BookWire's online index of book-related sites. If you schedule any author appearances, at bookstores or other events, send information about them to the Authors on the Highway section of BookWire (www.bookwire.com/highway).

You may also want to consider buying advertising space on other websites, where your potential bookbuyers are likely to be found. If you have a book on herbs, for example, you might buy a "banner ad," which would appear when someone accessed one of the online directories. You may also make a key word referral arrangement with one of the search engines, so that someone searching for "herbs" would be directed to your site.

Especially if your long-term plan is to develop a line of books in your chosen field, you will want people to come back to your website again and again. In that case, you will want to offer some material that will draw them back. That can be anything from a playful contest to a regularly updated list of events in your field to a superb list of the best websites in that field. Author-publisher Jim Donovan, for example, has a "Perk Up Your Day" daily message at the website for his book *Handbook to a Happier Life* (www.jimdonovan.com). At best, such material grows out of work you are already doing with your book or subject area. The hazard is that you will begin to provide material—such as updated statistics on your favorite tennis player—that take a great deal of time and effort to keep up. As a self-publisher, you should balance the time spent on such activities against the benefits to your promotion and selling; these can sometimes be hard to gauge directly, but just be sure the tail doesn't begin wagging the dog.

Beyond that, make sure you include your website address (also called a URL, or *Universal Resource Locator*) on all your promotional material. This includes your stationery, business cards, book jacket, copyright page of the book, and all advertisements.

If you are promoting or selling your book online in any way, be sure to keep a list of the e-mail addresses of prime people in the field, including possible buyers, reviewers, bulk orderers, and the like. If you are working in a special-interest area, sign up for and regularly participate in e-mail lists, forums, chat groups, newsgroups, listservs (mailing lists), and other kinds of online gatherings in your field. From all of these contacts, you can develop your own e-mail list of prime bookbuyers for books on topics in your field. Announcing a book via e-mail can be far less expensive than sending a direct-mail package. Internet etiquette frowns on the sending of bulk e-mail, but a specially tailored, select list can be a marvelous resource for your current and future books.

One interesting alternative approach to electronic publishing is that taken by Disc-Us Books, Inc. (www.disc-us.com); telephone: 888–695–9111. Disc-Us will contract for some or all of the electronic rights to your book or books, charge you a setup fee, and enter with you into what the organization describes as a "copublishing, comarketing venture." Disc-Us will take your work to market in a variety of ways over the Internet, starting with their own multi-author website, which will make sample pages or chapters of your work continually available for readers and potential bookbuyers, and fulfill copies of your work in either CD or print-on-demand book form. Royalties range from 20 percent to 50 percent of net receipts, on a sliding scale. As of this writing, the initial setup charge is $695, while the royalties are 20 percent of net receipts up to 500 sales, 40 percent on 500–2,500 copies, and 50 percent beyond that.

Other Selling Opportunities

Direct personal sales, book outlet sales, and mail sales are the three main ways you can sell your book. Many books can be sold in a variety of other ways as well, by reaching for definable audiences, nontraditional book outlets, and special book uses.

For example, a book on ski equipment may sell far better in ski equipment stores and ski industry catalogues than in bookstores and book catalogues. A book on French cheese may sell well in bookstores, but even better in specialty food outlets. A gun book may sell best in gun stores; a fishing book in sports equipment stores. These are all what the book trade calls "nontraditional" book outlets. A striking recent development in this sort of area is the computer store, which has been able to sell large quantities of computer books to computer buyers and users.

There are also special institutional uses. A book may be picked up and used as a premium, perhaps with a special cover and selling message on it. A book on personal income taxes may be used by a bank in this way; or a book on nutrition may be used as a premium by a food company anxious to show itself as public-spirited and a producer of nutritious, health-enhancing foods.

Clearly, many kinds of books do not offer such possibilities, such as most novels, works in medieval history, and satisfyingly obscure poetry. But some books will reach their audiences and make far larger sales in these "special markets," as they are called in the book trade, than through normal distribution channels.

If you have done a special-interest book that will sell well in a particular market, you are likely to already have a very good idea where to reach for specialty outlet sales and premium sales in the field. If you do not yet know, then talk to people in the field, perhaps the very same people you contacted while doing your book. Where there are chains to sell, approach them just as you would a bookstore chain—

and with the same caution. Where there are individual local stores to approach, make the same kind of personal selling approach you would with a bookstore.

Where there are companies using premiums as part of their marketing strategy, call into the home office, ask for the national marketing or sales department, and bounce about by telephone a bit until you find the right premium buyer to talk with. A caution on the premium sale, though: you may find yourself chasing a will-o'-the-wisp, with repeated callbacks and meetings with committees in company headquarters in some faraway city—and with no sale at the end of it all. Premium sales, as professionals in that field know, are all too often long drawn-out affairs, requiring expensive and time-consuming travel, repeated presentations, and protracted exposure to corporate bureaucracies. They seldom go well by telephone and mail; personal contact is usually necessary. If you do choose to try to sell your book as a premium, do your best to locate the right buyer, do as much as you can by telephone and letter, spend as little as you can, and don't get your hopes up prematurely. A big premium sale can be worth tens of thousands and sometimes hundreds of thousands of dollars, but don't let it distract you from the main chance, which is selling your self-published book in all the ways you can, to all the buyers you can find.

After the Sale

Like any other small manufacturer, the self-publishing author must also ship and bill goods that have been sold, and store inventory. Where cash or credit card orders have been received, as from individual mail order book buyers, the obligation is only to ship. Where you are dealing with institutions and booksellers, you will have to ship, bill, and quite often rebill.

You should certainly anticipate handling the billings yourself, although shipping and warehousing can be handled either directly or through a service organization. You will need the help of your accountant in setting up proper billing procedures and will certainly need help on the matter of which taxes to charge, geographically and by kind of sale.

Most self-publishers correctly choose to handle storing and shipping themselves. You can secure the services of one of the very competent and experienced fulfillment organizations advertising in *Literary Market Place*, but that is probably unnecessary and expensive. The truth is that it scarcely pays a fulfillment organization to set up a relationship with a self-publishing author doing a single book, unless that book takes off and becomes a substantial seller. And if that happens, and you do need fulfillment help, it is easy enough to secure later.

You will also ship more promptly if you handle it yourself. You can receive a single order and send it out the next day if you wish. Using someone else, you will have to send orders received on for fulfillment and wait your turn as orders are shipped; it will probably take a fulfillment organization two weeks longer to ship than it will take you. For control, speed, and economy, it is far better to do it yourself; if you need help, you can turn to family and friends, or hire a local teenager to work with you part-time, for much less than it would cost to use a fulfillment organization.

For shipping, you will need a supply of heavy kraft paper envelopes of a proper size for single copies of your book if it is light and soft-covered—for example, a small saddle-stitched book of poetry, or even a 160-page trade paperback. For heavier single books, you will need a standard padded envelope of the right size. Like the kraft envelopes, these are available from almost any substantial office supplies store or from office supply catalogues, often at a discount. Similar suppliers will also carry standard boxes in several sizes, capable of taking larger quantities of books, as when you send multiple copies to a bookseller; these can also be secured from industrial box companies.

You will also need standard shipping labels. It will probably pay to have a local printer print up some large self-adhesive labels with your return address and space for typing in at least six lines of address, so that you can use them for any international shipments you need to make, as well as for domestic shipments. You will also need standard stapling and taping tools and materials. Reinforced tape is advisable to keep the package securely closed.

For the actual shipping, your main choices are the U.S. Postal Service (USPS) and the United Parcel Service (UPS), as we discussed in Chapter 4. Shipping single copies via UPS costs more, but it is well worth considering. In the late 1990s, UPS is far more reliable and much, much faster than the federal postal system for these kinds of parcel deliveries. Postal service is slow and erratic; a book shipment may take anywhere from a couple of days to several weeks to get where it is going when the postal service handles it, while UPS consistently delivers the same book in a few days to a week. The time you save on handling complaints, the time and money you save in not having to reship "lost" orders that are just slow in arriving by mail, the ability to track shipments, and the willingness of booksellers to reorder when assured of prompt shipment should more than make up for the additional out-of-pocket costs you incur by shipping via UPS. Ship books by USPS only if you must.

You will be able to pick up standard multipart invoices for billing purposes and standard packing slips to include in shipments from an office supply store or catalogue. The invoice is your billing, with some parts kept for your internal use and for rebilling if necessary. The packing slip will contain some, but not all, of the same information contained on the invoice. Get your accountant to help you here, if you have no relevant business experience. What will take you hours of exploration—and perhaps result in expensive errors—will take any experienced accountant something like ten minutes in an office supply store. It is probably best to let your accountant pick up samples of the right invoices and packing slips from a store or some other client, bring them to you, tell you how to handle them, and work them into your bookkeeping system. You can then secure a full supply.

Should these standard invoices need a bit of adaptation for your needs, make sure that they include spaces for the date, your own invoice number, your customer's purchase order number, shipping and billing addresses (if books are to be billed and shipped to different places), author, title, price, discount if any, net price if different from price, and any shipping charges. You may want to give a 2 percent discount for bills paid within thirty days of the date on the invoice to encourage prompt payment; that is a standard commercial practice. If you can, get a multipart form that includes a packing slip; that slip should include all the information above, up to and including the title, and omit the pricing and billing information that follows.

You cannot expect bookstores to consistently reorder copies of your book when they come to what should be normal reorder points. Many bookstores do have excellent and reliable reorder systems, promptly reordering when stock goes down to a preset number of copies of a book. But such systems are as good as the people who work them, and even expensive computerized systems are no better than the data fed into them. It is wise to check your list of bookseller customers periodically, perhaps monthly, to see which ones have not reordered in the last few months and to call on those that are easily accessible while writing to the others and enclosing a reorder form. Selling more should also be part of post-sale activities.

Last—and a sore subject for authors, publishers, and booksellers alike—is the matter of returns. Standard practice in the book industry is to allow booksellers to return unsold new books to their publishers for full credit, or for refund of cash already paid if no other current billings are due, as is the case for most self-publishers. You will not be able to fight that, even though there are those who will advise you to try. Every large publisher plays by the same rules, allowing full return privileges; you will have to do the same.

Do not pay return shipping charges, though. Some large publishers may do so, but many do not—at least not yet. Aside from the cost to you, a store that has to pay to ship your book back to you may hold your book just a little longer, and sell it.

Your bookseller order form should carry your returns and discount policies as they apply to booksellers, and those policies should be firm. You might also attach or stamp your policies on your invoice. A fairly standard returns policy is one providing that books in good condition may be returned for full credit, starting ninety days after invoice date and no later than one year after that date.

These standard selling and fulfillment activities should allow you to develop the natural audience for most self-published books. Some books have wider potential, however, and in the next chapter we will explore ways to bring your books to much larger audiences if appropriate.

CHAPTER 7

....

Making the Most of Your Self-Published Book

Once created, it is possible for your self-published book to become a very considerable asset, far beyond the rewards coming directly from self-publication. You may publish it, achieve modestly successful sales, and then move it into major sales through republication with an alert commercial publisher. You may sell the subsidiary rights that it carries with it, in its status as both a book and a "property." You may use it to build valuable lists of direct-mail bookbuyers, bookseller customers, and friendly reviewers. Through your book, you can also build a considerable and very valuable reputation as an author and in some instances, therefore, as an expert.

Pickup by a Commercial Publisher

In Search of Excellence sold a decently successful 15,000 copies as a self-published book. Picked up by somebody alert to its possibilities at Harper and Row (now HarperCollins), it sold over a million copies in hardcover, becoming one of a very few all-time bestsellers. So, too, with a large and varied body of other self-published books, all the way from *Tarzan of the Apes* to *The First Whole Earth Catalog*.

All it really requires is a modicum of success in the marketplace as a self-published work, followed by a strong approach to commercial publishers, as many as you—or your agent—are willing to approach. That approach can be as indiscriminate as sending a letter and copy of your book to the president, appropriate divisional publisher, or chief editor of group after group of publishing companies, addressing each by name, pulled out of *Literary Market Place*. You can identify your best prospects—those companies that seem to be publishing the kind of book you have done—by studying the spring and fall announcements issues of *Publishers Weekly*, which carry the seasonal ads of most major publishers. You can also make a more targeted telephone or mail approach to a number of established agents, picked up out of the reasonably good listings of agents carried in *Literary Market Place*.

You can do it more carefully and probably far more effectively if you take the time to familiarize yourself somewhat with the publishing industry and its people before publishing your book. Six months of carefully reading *Publishers Weekly* will give what you need to see which publishers have recently had successes with self-publishing pickups. Similarly, scanning *Publishers Weekly*'s trade news articles will yield the names of dozens of very active agents, probably including several who have had recent successes with just your sort of book. Either way—blind or clear-eyed—your approach may bear fruit, for by the time you make that kind of approach, you have already put substantial investment into your work and have to some extent proven it in the marketplace. It is the rare commercial publisher, indeed, who will not give serious consideration to your kind of proposal, under those circumstances.

Subsidiary Rights

As a publishing "property," your book carries with it a body of *subsidiary rights*, which you may exercise or sell to others. The primary use is the form (or forms) in which you publish the work; other uses are labeled *subsidiary* to this use. When you publish a hardcover edition of your book, that is the primary use; paperback rights sold to a commercial publisher are a subsidiary use. But if you had published the book first in paperback, then your sale of hardcover rights would be a subsidiary sale.

Because of the diversity of special contacts required, it is desirable to have an agent handle subsidiary rights sales, rather than trying to do them yourself—unless, of course, you have some relevant experience and think you would like to try. It may be helpful to point out that commercial publishers see "rights" as a lucrative major specialty, as do larger agencies, and employ special marketing people to handle them.

Once your book is published, it should not be too difficult to get an agent to handle both commercial publisher pickup possibilities and "rights" sales, provided that your book is the kind of work that lends itself to such sales. A book of poetry or a narrow-market professional book may not offer enough rights possibilities to get agent attention—or for that matter to engage much of your own attention in selling rights. But a hardcover that might do well in paperback, a novel that might adapt well for the screen, or a work that might sell well around the world, perhaps in many languages, all are prime rights candidates. You should make a very serious attempt to sell those rights, preferably through agents or, if necessary, on your own. In many instances, rights sales have yielded far more revenue and the resulting works have reached far wider audiences than the original work.

Here are the main kinds of possible rights sales:

- *Paperback rights*: Assuming that you have published first in hardcover, the right to publish in trade or mass market paperback can be sold to someone else. This sale usually follows hardcover publication, sometimes many months and even years later, after your book has sold well in hardcover. If you do sell paperback rights, be sure to specify at least a year between original publication and paperback publication, in order to safeguard your higher-priced hardcover sales. Of course, that would not apply if your sale is for the purpose of replacing your self-published hardcover with a much more widely distributed commercial publisher's paperback edition, or your paperback with their hardcover.

- *Book club rights:* A book club may publish its own edition of your work or purchase multiple copies from you as a publisher. Major clubs, such as the Book-of-the-Month Club and the Literary Guild, usually require prepublication copies of your work—but call and ask, for policies can change. Sending advance copies to such clubs can become very worthwhile. Other smaller book clubs prefer prepublication copies, but will often accept finished books arriving before your official publication date, and may accept books received long after. If you do not have an agent, you may have to go to book clubs on your own, at least the major ones.

- *First serialization:* This is the right to run part—or all, but that is rare—of your work in a periodical, almost always prepublication. It does not pay very much, but can be wonderful free advertising and third-party recommendation.

- *Second serialization:* This is really second and any subsequent serializations, often occurring post-publication. This can pay a good deal in a major newspaper or national magazine, sometimes as much as tens of thousands of dollars, though these kinds of bonanza serialization fees are few and far between.

- *Screen and other dramatizations:* This covers sale of your work or any part of it, such as its name, for use in movies, television, radio, stage, videodisk, or any similar forms. Fiction is most often so sold, but nonfiction has also often been sold for dramatizations as well as for the development of documentary films. This, of course, is the largest bonanza rights area of all. It is the rare novelist, indeed, who does not secretly see his or her work as, in screen terms, another *Dodsworth, Gone With the Wind, Ragtime,* or *Jurassic Park.*

- *Foreign and translation rights:* Foreign rights usually means English language rights in other countries, while translation usually means sale of rights to put the work into other languages. This is something you should do yourself only with great trepidation. Some agents advertise themselves as specializing in this kind of rights sale, though most well-established agents will handle foreign and translation rights.

- *Condensation and adaptation rights:* These are seldom worth a great deal—but the right work in the hands of the right seller can result in a $20,000 or more condensation sale to Reader's Digest Condensed Books, or a smallish but potentially lucrative adaptation sale to someone wanting to convert your adult book into a children's book.

- *Computerized database, CD-ROM, microform, etc.:* Modern technology has spawned a grab bag of miscellaneous forms with a growing series of rights that can be sold to others, usually for very little money. This is a still-changing field, with new forms still emerging, and it is unclear which forms—perhaps some not yet in existence—will be most valuable in the long run.

The main comment to make here is defensive: no one really yet understands where publishing and publishing forms are going in this era of very quickly developing publishing, broadcasting, and computer technology. Some of these forms may be a substantial portion of the "books" of the future. If you sell any rights to anyone, be very sure that these kinds of rights are not simply given away in the fine print of the contract. *The key thing to understand in selling rights is that you must be paid for any rights you convey to others, specifically by the kinds of rights conveyed.* Note that if you do succeed in making any kind of rights sale on your own but have no experience in this area, you would be wise to have an experienced agent negotiate the contract for you; you can be badly hurt otherwise. Once a sale has been made, very few agents will hesitate to handle it for you, even if it is rather small; the agent will then also see other possibilities. And the 15–20 percent you will pay the agent will be entirely worth it to you.

Self-publishers who successfully sell their books by direct mail may also be building up a substantial additional asset in the form of the mailing list they develop. A few hundred direct-mail bookbuyers will not do much for you, but if you have a list composed of a few thousand or more bookbuyers on your specific subject, you may be able to rent it again and again, if you place it in the hands of a list broker. A list of 5,000 book buyers may be worth no more than $200 per rental, and perhaps only $100–$150 of that to you, once you subtract the percentage charged by the list broker and the cost of providing it to the renter. But if you do more than one book, and therefore continue to update and probably expand your list, it may come to be worth several thousands of dollars a year in rentals. This is all purely incremental income; it requires no significant additional effort or expenditure on your part, because you are promoting your books to that list anyway.

Most direct-mail sellers rent the lists they develop, some netting large profits by doing so; so should self-publishers. You will find large list brokers specializing in books in *Literary Market Place*; by listing themselves there, they have conveniently identified themselves for you. Mailing consultants are also listed, but comparative shopping of your list among large brokers should suffice.

The lists of bookseller customers and friendly reviewers you develop have no similar direct economic uses, but are valuable to the extent that you can use them to distribute other books.

Building Your Reputation

An author who sells well builds a reputation, with or without a substantial body of personal promotional activities. But, as previously discussed, your book is likely to sell a lot better if you push it hard in every way you can, with great energy and without undue modesty.

The bonus you can get from promoting your book in this way is enhanced reputation, which proceeds from both increasing your audience and letting that audience see you and come to respect what you have to say. Many a lecture-circuit, traveling-seminar, or television career—usually a combination of all three—has started with a single book. A grueling book promotion tour sponsored by a commercial publisher may be helpful for quick exposure, but a more deliberate personal campaign, which increases your audience and reputation as you expand your book's audience and sales, may do more for both you and your book in the long run.

By all means do it all, unless you suffer from critically disabling shyness that somehow cannot be overcome. Read your poetry; lecture to consumers and colleagues all over the country; develop a corporate seminar with your book as text and centerpiece; aggressively pursue local cable television, so hungry for programming; teach a local extension course and then move on to the local community college; become a personality, a guru, a celebrity. In America now, celebrity pays. Of course, celebrity has nothing to do with creating either art or clean expository writing—but it can help sell books, earn fees, and settle you into an authoring career, as such careers are built in the United States today.

Having taken the potential self-publisher from idea through finished book, to market and beyond, we have completed the main body of this work, keenly aware that there is—as always when briefly discussing a whole profession and set of industries—much more that can be said. We hope this book has effectively introduced all the main matters connected with self-publishing and that it incorporates enough of the main sources of help in the field to make it possible for an author to understand the right questions, avoid the main pitfalls, and go ahead to self-publish a book.

Now follow a discussion and listing of some main reference tools and sources, and a glossary of some of the main terms encountered in self-publishing. The index will give more specific references to discussion of various terms in the text. Also included here is a list of standard proofreading and editing marks, with examples of how they are used in editing manuscript, marking manuscript for composition, and making corrections or changes on proof; a flow chart of the publishing process; samples of common book types; and a sample press release.

APPENDIX 1

Sources of Information

People planning to publish their own work will find many large bodies of published information to draw upon. All kinds of people offering professional help, tens of thousands of booksellers and librarians, and millions of names on mailing lists can be easily reached through the Internet and many standard works of reference. Scores of books exist that together cover every aspect of publishing, including at least two score devoted to self-publishing.

The wealth of material available stems from the nature of the publishing industry itself, which is full of people who quite normally and predictably tend to write and publish about what they know best—their own industry. Indeed, no other industry as small as publishing has generated such a body of information sources. And it is a small industry, by the way; for all its supposed glamour many individual American corporations are far larger than the entire publishing industry, even including the periodical portion.

Insight is always much harder to achieve than information, however. A beginning self-publisher may wade through many publications of all kinds, speak to many of the wrong people, and never find the right sources to develop insight and information.

You will start best by seeking other self-publishers, people who have gone through it all before you, and who have—perhaps rather painfully—learned how to ask the right questions about self-publishing and to avoid the worst pitfalls along the way. You are likely to find other self-publishers—and for that matter most small publishers, whether they publish their own work or the work of others—very willing to talk to you. Most will tell you about their experiences; recommend, or warn you away from, freelancers, printers, and suppliers of all kinds; discuss marketing techniques; and in short treat you as a new member of their "club." For many, that is exactly what it is—a national and international fraternity of small publishers, drawn together by a shared love of writing and books and thinking of itself very much as a "movement." Many will speak of it as the small press movement and quite consciously welcome you into it.

You will be able to find some of them locally through a bookseller who acts as informal clearinghouse and carries many local small-press books. You will find others through local special-interest circles, and simply by word of mouth, once you begin to ask around. You will find others—thousands of others, some of whom will turn out to be local and unknown to you—through some standard sources that follow here. Some of those you most want to listen to will be writing in or interviewed in some of the periodicals listed.

But small press movement or not, publishing is publishing. If you want to learn enough to publish and market your book well and cost-effectively, you had best learn to use the tools of the trade. You will profit greatly every step of the way—especially if you want to take your self-published book out into the wider worlds of commercial and international publishing—by using such publisher's tools as *Literary Market Place*, *Publishers Weekly*, and the others we list and discuss below.

Most of the large reference books and periodicals listed here are to be found in local libraries, and certainly in large regional libraries, as they are extensively used by the public and as librarian's tools. A few of these large and often expensive works may be worth buying, despite their prices. The smaller works discussed here are, as of this writing, all in print and can be purchased, though some are found in a few libraries.

Here then are a group of published sources—selected from the otherwise possibly bewildering body of works available—that we consider very useful for people who want to publish their own works.

Literary Market Place (LMP), published annually by R. R. Bowker Co., 121 Chanlon Road, New Providence, NJ 07974; 800–521–8110; (www.bowker.com). As of this writing, *Literary Market Place* was preparing to open a website (www.literarymarketplace.com). It planned to offer *LMP* on a subscription basis, though some portions (including service listings) would be available free.

For most self-publishers, *LMP* is very much worth buying, or subscribing to online, although it is increasingly expensive. It is far and away the best source of practical publishing help available. If it did not exist, the book you are now reading would have to be at least twice as long to attempt to list even a smallish fraction of the basic material covered.

Literary Market Place provides all kinds of key information, services, and suppliers, including:

- *U.S. and Canadian publishers,* including a separate section on *small presses.*

- *Printers and manufacturers,* many of whom advertise themselves as handling short runs and providing complete post-editorial services. It also supplies paper merchants and mills, though you are unlikely to order your paper directly.

- *Editorial services,* of all kinds, from those doing single functions to those offering to take your book all the way from idea to finished manuscript. Many of these are also quite ready to shepherd your book all the way through the production process to finished books as well. *LMP* indexes editorial services by kind of service offered.

- *Artists and art services,* also indexed by kind of service offered; many of these offer complete book design and layout services.

- *Direct mail services* of all kinds, also indexed, and including brokers, printers, mailers, and mailing package creators.

- *Electronic publishing* consultants, products, and services.

- Many more kinds of services and suppliers, including *indexers, book exhibitors* at meetings and conventions, *photographers, shippers, translators, word processors, bookbinders, consultants, public relations services,* and *advertising agencies,* among others.

The great virtue of *Literary Market Place* in regard to suppliers of all kinds is that the listings are self-selecting. Every person or organization listed here wants to do business with publishers and holds itself out as experienced in doing that kind of business. If you comparison-shop a book manufacturing or mailing job out of *LMP,* you are quite likely to find somebody who will do your work well and competitively; if you do so in your local area, you may find no one proper to work with, and probably won't even know it, being inexperienced yourself. If you seek editorial help out of *LMP,* rather than out of the local community college English department, you are likely to find competent, and sometimes superb, help. The same is true for every category; this is the prime source for American book publishing.

LMP also contains substantial lists of *literary agents,* including most full-time and active American agents.

It is also a prime source from which you can compile a *reviewer's list,* as it carries substantial lists of key book reviewers in all print and broadcast media. In practical terms, you will usually need only to add local and special interest publication reviewers to make up your reviewer's list.

LMP also carries a list of many *book clubs,* to which you will want to try to sell subsidiary rights to your book.

There is more: *LMP* carries a very substantial list of national and regional *distributors,* so important to many self-publishers, and an even longer list of *wholesalers.*

It also carries a list of the country's main *remainder wholesalers,* should you ultimately need to dispose of overstock.

It carries listings of a wide selection of periodicals and reference works, covering every aspect of publishing and its related fields.

In a separate volume, *LMP* includes a Yellow Pages section, carrying the names, addresses, and telephone numbers of thousands of people listed under their organizations in the book.

Publishers Weekly, also published by Bowker. This is the single most important publishing industry periodical published in the United States. If you want to give yourself a short course in practical publishing as part of the self-publishing process—and you should want to do so—then immerse yourself in *Publishers Weekly* over a year's subscription. Most aspects of publishing, large and small, are covered in any year, with special issues devoted to spring and fall book announcements, and special issues throughout the year devoted to several kinds of special-interest publishing and to particular markets. If you cannot see your way clear to buying a subscription, then go to the library every week and spend at least an hour reading the publication from cover to cover. Almost every library of moderate size will have a subscription, though you may have to ask for it and pry it away from the librarians themselves, because it is a prime librarian's tool as well as a prime publisher's tool.

It is far better to subscribe, though. Then you can relate articles, clip and copy, and build up a file relating to your publishing needs and interests. You can also then go back and reread. What seemed unimportant at one point may seem vital a little later on as you move through the publishing process.

Whether you read at home or in the library, make sure that you follow several kinds of continuing matters, as well as the content of special issues and of leading articles of interest.

- Follow the news sections. Although much will seem irrelevant for you, together they will tell much about what is being published in your area of interest, what is doing well and why, and what you can expect when you move out into the marketplace to do business. Coverage on rights sales will tell you a great deal about which books are being sold to whom and by whom for what kinds of subsidiary rights. It will also identify for you many active agents, some general and some specialist, who can be called upon to handle your book when the time comes to move it beyond its basic self-publishing form into other print and broadcast forms, and abroad.

- Follow the book design and manufacturing section, which often covers matters of interest to small publishers, as when it covers printers using new production processes that make short runs cheaper—and therefore more attractive—than ever before.

- Follow the advertisements—all of them. Together, they will tell you how publishers are going about selling books to booksellers, with what offers and in what formats, which suppliers are stressing their small press capabilities, what new mailing lists and valuable sources of information are available, and a great deal more.

Publishers Weekly gives you all of this, and a good deal more, including new legal pitfalls as they develop, bestsellers, and a large body of book reviews. In short, every publisher—and especially a neophyte publisher, who will get the most from it—should read it with great care.

Small Press: The Magazine of Independent Publishing, published bi-monthly; Jenkins Group, 121 East Front Street, Traverse City, MI 49684; 616-933-0445 (www.bookpublishing.com). This magazine is aimed directly at small press publishers, including self-publishers.

BookWire (www.bookwire.com), a website to which various partners contribute, including publications such as *Publishers Weekly* and *Library Journal,* and organizations such as the Association of Authors' Representatives, the Book Industry Study Group, and the National Book Foundation. It offers online current news, events, and reviews in publishing, as well as features on authors and publishers, all of which you can examine for tips in preparing your own publishing plans. Most helpfully, it provides links to more than 7,000 publishing industry sites on the Internet, including publishers, booksellers, libraries, authors, book sites, trade organizations and associations, wholesalers and distributors, writing resources, editorial and production services, marketing services, review sources, book-related news-groups, and other resources. You can readily add your own listing to their index of links.

The International Directory of Little Magazines and Small Presses, published annually by Dustbooks, P.O. Box 100, Paradise, CA; 800-477-6110 or 530-877-6110; (www.dustbooks.com). This prime source will help you to locate small press publishers in your own area, including those sharing your kind of publishing interests; it carries subject and regional indexes.

Bookmaking: The Illustrated Guide to Design/Production/Editing, by Marshall Lee, published by W. W. Norton, 500 Fifth Avenue, New York, NY 10110; 212-354-5500; (www.wwnorton.com). We highly recommend this excellent work, which covers every significant aspect of design, production, and editing. It is intended for beginning and working professionals in these fields, but is written so clearly that any beginning self-publisher, with no experience in these areas, will profit greatly from reading and using it. It also contains an excellent bibliography.

American Book Trade Directory, published annually by Bowker. This is the most complete and up-to-date directory available, covering more than 31,000 American and Canadian bookstores, distributors, and wholesalers, and other bookselling organizations and people, and carrying such vital information as kinds of books and buyers by name. It serves as the basis for Bowker's bookstore and wholesaler mailing lists, which may be rented, should you wish to make direct selling mailings to bookstores and wholesalers. You should find this directory available in many moderate-sized and all large regional libraries.

Note that you need not rent the Bowker lists, especially if you want to do small local or regional mailings, or to compile a small, complete prospect list of bookstores and wholesalers you want to call on personally. Then you can work directly from a library copy of the directory.

American Library Directory, published annually by Bowker. This is an up-to-date directory of more than 37,000 American and Canadian libraries of all kinds, broken down in several ways, including size of bookbuying budget and kinds of materials purchased. It serves as the basis for Bowker's library mailing lists, which—like the bookstore and wholesaler lists derived from the book trade directory—may be rented. You may want to do some targeted special mailings out of the book or the rented lists, even while relying upon specialist library jobbers for the main library sales of your book. It is available in most libraries, as it is a prime librarian's tool.

Standard Periodical Directory, published annually by Oxbridge Communications, Inc., 150 Fifth Avenue, New York, NY 10011; 800–955–0231; (www.mediafinder.com). This is a standard advertising industry tool available in most libraries. It will supply the basic information you need to place advertising, should you decide to go into such publications as special-interest magazines on your own. Computer users should note that Oxbridge's website is handy for developing a quick list of periodicals related to specific topics. Note that we feel it much better to do such placements through an agency or freelancer who "knows the ropes"; doing so can save the inexperienced some costly errors.

Audiovisual Market Place, published annually by Bowker. This is the audiovisual industry equivalent of *Literary Market Place* and is found in most libraries. You will find it quite useful if you want to include an audiovisual component in your work.

International Literary Market Place, published annually by Bowker. This is an international publishing equivalent of *Literary Market Place* and will be useful should you decide to try to handle the sale of international rights or set up international distribution arrangements on your own, as it carries the key people and organizations you will want to reach.

Among the various professional associations, you may want to explore two nationwide organizations for small or independent publishers.

One is the Small Publishers Association of North America (SPAN), P.O. Box 1306, Buena Vista, CO 81211; 719-395-4790, Fax: 719–395–8374; e-mail: span@SPANnet.org (www.SPANnet.org). The other is the Publishers Marketing Association, 627 Aviation Way, Manhattan Beach, CA 90266; 310–372–2732, Fax: 310–374–3342; e-mail: info@pma-online.org (www.pma-online.org). Both of these organizations have newsletters.

Computer users will find the websites for both organizations valuable. PMA, for example, offers online resource directories, member directories, newsletters, calendars of book expositions, and information about various marketing programs. SPAN offers information on advertising opportunities, publishing events, partners, and literary links, as well as a book emporium. Websites are constantly changing, but perusing these and other such sites will help you assess what they have to offer and decide whether or not to become a member, as each offers some benefits to members only.

You also may want to consider joining the Author's Guild at 330 West 42nd Street, 29th Floor, New York, NY 10036; 212–563–5904; (www.authorsguild.org), especially if you have published at least one book already. Although much of the guild's attention is focused on the relationships between authors and commercial publishing houses, they provide much useful information and guidance on questions of copyright, libel, invasion of privacy, and the like, both in the initial packet of materials sent to new members and in the quarterly *Author's Guild Bulletin*.

APPENDIX 2

The Self-Publishing Process

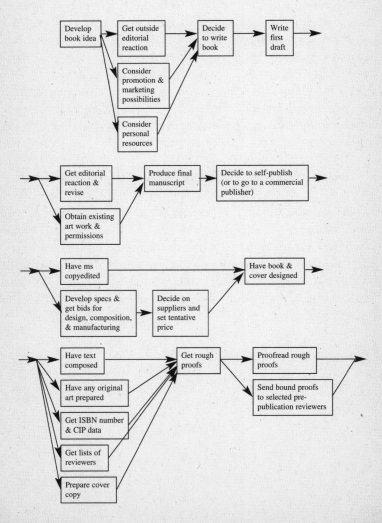

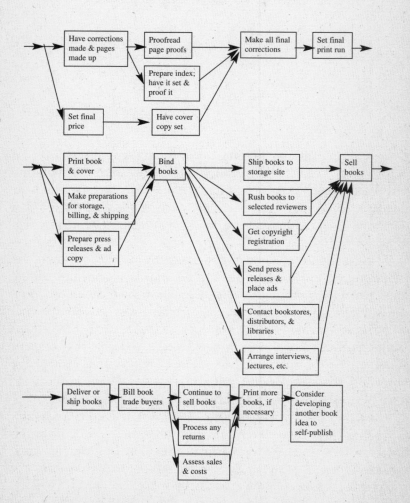

APPENDIX 3

....

Copyediting and
Proofreading Marks

Copyediting and proofreading marks form a special small sublanguage by which authors, editors, and compositors communicate with each other. Over the centuries they have become relatively standardized, so that even strangers, working together for the first time, can specify with assurance details of format so essential to each work.

These marks are used somewhat differently at various stages in the publishing process. During the writing and developmental editing stage, when the work is generally in double-spaced manuscript form, copyediting marks are generally made in the spaces between the lines or in the wide margins of the page. This is the stage where the manuscript receives its heaviest editing. Indeed, although some inexperienced writers expect to produce clean copy first crack out of the typewriter, the manuscripts of most professional writers at this stage resemble nothing so much as battle maps.

Once the developmental editing is finished and a final typescript is produced, the copy editor does a much lighter editing of manuscript. At this stage, the aims are to correct any lingering inconsistencies in the manuscript and to specify necessary details of format to compositors, a process often called *typemarking*.

Proofreading is handled somewhat differently. After the manuscript has been composed, proofs are read for typographical errors or errors of format. Inevitably, too, other kinds of errors emerge on this proofreading, for the manuscript always looks different—no matter how experienced the eye—when it is set in type. But this is no longer double-spaced manuscript with room for changes between the lines.

For clarity and accuracy, all changes and corrections at the proofreading stage are made in the margins to the left or right of each line; if multiple changes are to be made on a line, they are separated in the margins by diagonal lines (*virgules*). Only marks indicating where changes are to be made appear in the body of the text, and are always flagged in the margin, to be sure they are not overlooked by the compositor as the corrections are being made. Authors—and especially author-publishers—should carefully mark their changes either PE (Printer's Error) or AA (Author's Alteration), since the charges for these may be in dispute if the amount of changes is large.

Following is a table of the main copyediting and proofreading marks in use today, and then a brief example of how these marks are used in marking the same piece of copy at the three main stages mentioned above.

Copyediting and Proofreading Marks

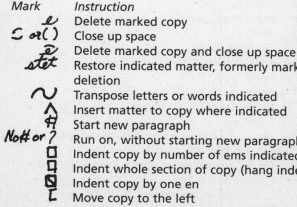

Mark	Instruction
l	Delete marked copy
⊂ or ( )	Close up space
e	Delete marked copy and close up space
stet	Restore indicated matter, formerly marked for deletion
∼	Transpose letters or words indicated
∧	Insert matter to copy where indicated
¶	Start new paragraph
No¶ or ?	Run on, without starting new paragraph
☐	Indent copy by number of ems indicated
☐	Indent whole section of copy (hang indent)
☐	Indent copy by one en
⌐	Move copy to the left

⅃	Move copy to the right
⅃⌐	Center copy in column or image area
⊓	Move copy higher
⊔	Move copy lower
＝	Align type horizontally
‖	Align type vertically
#	Insert space
Eq #	Equalize spacing
Sp	Spell out
——	Set underlined copy in italic type
∿∿∿	Set underlined copy in boldface type
∿∿∿	Set underlined copy in boldface italic type
rom	Reset indicated copy in roman type
Ital	Reset indicated copy in italic type
bf	Reset indicated copy in boldface type
bf *ital*	Reset indicated copy in boldface italic type
≡	Set in large capital letters
≡	Set in small capital letters
≡ ≡	Set first letter in large capitals, rest in small
/	Change capital letter to lower case
	(also used to separate changes in copy margins or text)
?	Double-check matter
⊙	Insert period
⋏	Insert comma
ⱽ	Insert apostrophe
⁙	Insert quotation marks
ⱽ	Insert superscript
⋀	Insert subscript
⋏	Insert semicolon
⊙	Insert colon
=or-ᑕ	Insert hyphen
⊥ₘ	Insert an em dash
⊥ₙ	Insert an en dash
# *or ld*	Insert space (*leading*) between lines
lig	Use ligature (combined letters, such as æ), where indicated
⟳	Move encircled copy to indicated spot
(out...see copy)	Pick-up copy omitted in composition
⬭	Do not set encircled comments to editor or compositor
hr #	Leave hair space between letters
•••• *or* •••	Insert ellipses where material was cut from quotation

Copyediting and Proofreading Marks

Manuscript in Development

Chapter ~~Ten~~ 10

T~~H~~E INCENSE ROAD

~~1~~ And when the queen of Sheba heard of the fame
of Solomon...

~~2~~ she came to Jerusalem with a very great train,
with camels that bare spices, and very much gold, and
precious stones...

~~10 And she gave the king an hundred and twenty talents...~~

I: 1-10
(~~I~~ Kings)

On her way to the l~~n~~a~~d~~ of Israe~~l~~y, the Queen of Sheba
followed the old Incense Road, which ~~brought~~ carried spices and
other goods ~~desired for religious use~~ north from Arabia, --one of early to the great kingdoms
along the Mediterranean Sea, --

stet For over 1500 miles the ~~caravan~~ trail wound through ~~rocky~~ rock-bound
~~desert~~ gorges from the Hadramaht to Jordan and Syria.

Manuscript in Copyediting and Typemarking:

> And when the queen of Sheba heard of the fame of Solomon...she came to Jerusalem with a very great train, with camels that bare spices, and very much gold, and precious stones...
>
> (Kings I: 1/10)

On her way to the land of Israel—one of the many great early kingdoms along the Mediterranean Sea—the queen of Sheba followed the old Incense Road, which carried spices and other goods north from Arabia.

For over 1500 miles the caravan trail wound through rock-bound gorges from the Hadramaut to Jordan and Syria.

Proofs for Corrections

CHAPTER TEN

THE INCENSE ROAD

And when the queen of Sheba heard of the fame of Solomon . . . she came to Jerusalem with a very great train, with camels that bare spices, and very much gold, and precious stones

(I Kings: 1-2)

On her way to the land of Israel—one of the many great early kingdoms along the Mediterranean Sea—the Queen of Sheba followed the old Incense Road, which carried spices and other goods north from Arabia.

For over 1500 miles the caravan trail wound through rockbound gorges from the Hadramaut to Jordan and Syria.

APPENDIX 4

....

Type Specimen Sheet

TIMES ROMAN

ABCDEFGHIJKLMNOPQRSTUVWXYZ
abcdefghijklmnopqrstuvwxyz $1234567890

When choosing a type for your book, you will look at type specimen sheets, like this one, showing the basic font of the type and a sample of text in print. Before making a final choice, have at least one full page set in your desired type, so you can be sure it is readable in large blocks.

HELVETICA

ABCDEFGHIJKLMNOPQRSTUVWXYZ
abcdefghijklmnopqrstuvwxyz $1234567890

When choosing a type for your book, you will look at type specimen sheets, like this one, showing the basic font of the type and a sample of text in print. Before making a final choice, have at least one full page set in your desired type, so you can be sure it is readable in large blocks.

OPTIMA

ABCDEFGHIJKLMNOPQRSTUVWXYZ
abcdefghijklmnopqrstuvwxyz $1234567890

When choosing a type for your book, you will look at type specimen
sheets, like this one, showing the basic font of the type and a sample
of text in print. Before making a final choice, have at least one full
page set in your desired type, so you can be sure it is readable in large
blocks.

KORINNA

ABCDEFGHIJKLMNOPQRSTUVWXYZ
abcdefghijklmnopqrstuvwxyz $1234567890

When choosing a type for your book, you will look at type specimen sheets, like this one, showing the basic font of the type and
a sample of text in print. Before making a final choice, have at
least one full page set in your desired type, so you can be sure it
is readable in large blocks.

BODONI

ABCDEFGHIJKLMNOPQRSTUVWXYZ
abcdefghijklmnopqrstuvwxyz $1234567890

When choosing a type for your book, you will look at type specimen
sheets, like this one, showing the basic font of the type and a sample of
text in print. Before making a final choice, have at least one full page
set in your desired type, so you can be sure it is readable in large
blocks.

JANSON

ABCDEFGHIJKLMNOPQRSTUVWXYZ
abcdefghijklmnopqrstuvwxyz $1234567890

When choosing a type for your book, you will look at type specimen sheets, like this one, showing the basic font of the type and a sample of text in print. Before making a final choice, have at least one full page set in your desired type, so you can be sure it is readable in large blocks.

JANSON ITALIC

ABCDEFGHIJKLMNOPQRSTUVWXYZ
abcdefghijklmnopqrstuvwxyz $1234567890

When choosing a type for your book, you will look at type specimen sheets, like this one, showing the basic font of the type and a sample of text in print. Before making a final choice, have at least one full page set in your desired type, so you can be sure it is readable in large blocks.

MELIOR

ABCDEFGHIJKLMNOPQRSTUVWXYZ
abcdefghijklmnopqrstuvwxyz $1234567890

When choosing a type for your book, you will look at type specimen sheets, like this one, showing the basic font of the type and a sample of text in print. Before making a final choice, have at least one full page set in your desired type, so you can be sure it is readable in large blocks.

GARAMOND

ABCDEFGHIJKLMNOPQRSTUVWXYZ
abcdefghijklmnopqrstuvwxyz $1234567890

When choosing a type for your book, you will look at type specimen sheets, like this one, showing the basic font of the type and a sample of text in print. Before making a final choice, have at least one full page set in your desired type, so you can be sure it is readable in large blocks.

ELECTRA

ABCDEFGHIJKLMNOPQRSTUVWXYZ
abcdefghijklmnopqrstuvwxyz $1234567890

When choosing a type for your book, you will look at type specimen sheets, like this one, showing the basic font of the type and a sample of text in print. Before making a final choice, have at least one full page set in your desired type, so you can be sure it is readable in large blocks.

APPENDIX 5

....

Sample Press Release

NEWS
FROM

"*Superbly selected and annotated, the* **AMERICAN HERITAGE** DICTIONARY OF
AMERICAN QUOTATIONS *brims with the wisdom and witticisms of our ancestors while
also honoring our most noteworthy contemporary commentators. Easily the best book of
American quotations ever compiled.*"

> --Douglas Brinkley, Director, The Eisenhower Center for American Studies and
> Professor of History, University of New Orleans.

"*The* **AMERICAN HERITAGE** DICTIONARY OF AMERICAN QUOTATIONS *belongs
on every history buff's bookshelf. An invaluable reference guide to better understanding our
great nation.*"

> --Stephen E. Ambrose, author of *D-Day* and *Undaunted Courage: Thomas Jefferson,
> Meriweather Lewis and the Opening of the West*

A selection of the History Book Club.

AMERICAN HERITAGE
DICTIONARY OF AMERICAN
QUOTATIONS

Selected and Annotated by

Margaret Miner and Hugh Rawson

The **AMERICAN HERITAGE** DICTIONARY OF AMERICAN QUOTATIONS

(Penguin Reference, January 3, 1997, $29.95, 656 pp), selected and annotated by

Margaret Miner and Hugh Rawson, is not merely a comprehensive collection of

thoughts and sayings, but also a portrait of American life and culture. Including more

than 5,000 quotes on over 500 topics, this highly readable reference records the national

experience as viewed by Americans from all walks of life.

Organized in a browser-friendly, single-column format, with quotations chosen not only for their historical significance but with an eye to their future utility, the book incorporates two helpful features that distinguish the **AMERICAN HERITAGE** DICTIONARY OF AMERICAN QUOTATIONS from other collections of quotations: First, the extensive annotations which follow approximately thirty percent of the quotes, setting them in historical context. And secondly, the chronological method of organization within subjects, allowing readers to trace key historical sequences and demonstrating how the views of the nation on particular topics have changed and developed over time.

Complete with cross references as well as author and keyword indexes, the **AMERICAN HERITAGE** DICTIONARY OF AMERICAN QUOTATIONS serves as an invaluable new reference guide that offers insight into how Americans see America.

ABOUT THE EDITORS

Margaret Miner and Hugh Rawson are also the editors of *The New International Dictionary of Quotations, A Dictionary of Quotations from the Bible*, and *A Dictionary of Quotations from Shakespeare*. On his own, Hugh Rawson is the author of *Wicked Words, Devious Derivations*, and *Rawson's Dictionary of Euphemisms & Other Doubletalk*. They live in Roxbury, Connecticut.

# # #

AMERICAN HERITAGE DICTIONARY OF AMERICAN QUOTATIONS

Selected and Annotated by Margaret Miner and Hugh Rawson

Publication Date: January 3, 1997

Price: $29.95

For further information, please contact Roel Torres at Viking Publicity 212/366-2224.

GLOSSARY

··

In any new field, learning the language is often half the battle. The language of publishing can be rather daunting to self-publishing authors, who often feel as if they were drowning in a sea of unfamiliar terms, especially when dealing with production and editorial people. Here then is a relatively brief selection of such commonly encountered special terms, arranged and related for easy understanding. Where a term has been discussed in the main text of this book in more detail, or is better set in context there, we say so, referring you to the chapter in which it is discussed. The index will indicate precise page references.

addenda, errata, corrigenda: The book world still uses many words like these, left over from the Latin and Greek that were for so long the main languages of educated Europeans. In some instances, they are not even leftovers, but instead pretentious pseudo-Latin terms. These three are merely jargon, with clear modern English equivalents; you need to know what they mean, rather than use them in your book, for they are sometimes confusingly used as synonyms. *Addenda* are brief additions to an already printed book, pasted or otherwise fixed onto an already bound book or bound into a printed but as yet unbound book. *Errata* are errors, likewise affixed or bound in. *Corrigenda* is a synonym for *errata*.

author's alterations (AAs), printer's errors (PEs): These terms raise the ever-vexing question of who did what to the manuscript during the composition process and who will pay for changes. *Author's alterations*—called AAs in the publishing and printing trades—are any changes made by the author on composed type after initial composition, except for those correcting errors made by compositors in setting type from manuscript, which are called PEs, for *printer's errors*. Your contract with a compositor should allow for some AAs without additional charges, and additional AAs at stated hourly—rather than per-page—charges. Note that if you are allowed, for example, 10 percent of total initial composition costs for no-charge AAs, that does not mean that 10 percent of the words in the manuscript can be altered without additional charges, for alterations cost more per word or character to do than initial composition. Rather, alterations will be charged at the agreed-upon rate, with all charges under 10 percent of the original cost being absorbed by the printer and the balance being paid for by you, the author-publisher. As you read and correct page proofs, note which corrections are AAs and which PEs on both the master set you return to the compositor and the copy you keep. You may need that information later if you feel that you may have been overcharged on AAs.

blueprints: The several kinds of blue, silver, brown, and other prints are fully discussed in Chapter 5.

book face: Any typeface thought by a book's designer to be suitable for a particular book may be described as a book face. Normally, though, a printer, designer, or editor means by this a typeface that has enough size and body to look good and be easy to read when used in a book. Typewriter faces, for example, may look good on a manuscript page, because of their size and spacing, but work very badly when used in books, because they are too large to use full size and too thin and hard to read when reduced for book page use. At the other extreme, some typefaces used in newspapers may be suitable for a fast scan or quick read but too small and dense for use in books.

book size, trim size: A whole body of nomenclature, mostly archaic, applies to book sizes, all based upon the way sheets coming off presses of certain sizes were folded and the page sizes that resulted.

For modern American publishing purposes, it suffices to know that book size refers to the size of the trimmed pages of the book, rather than to the size of the covers of the book, and that sizes are described in inches. Hardcovers and trade paperbacks composed mainly of text normally run from about 5" x 7" to 7" x 10" in trimmed page size, while heavily illustrated books more often run in the 8½" x 11" and 9" x 12" range, with some running even larger. Mass market paperbacks, and even some small hardcovers, go down into the 4¼"x 7" range, with some novelty sizes going much smaller. Should anyone begin to discuss book sizes in terms of folios, quartos, octavos, and the like, ask that the discussion be carried on in modern terms.

bullets, boxes, fists, arrows, flags, and the rest: These are a whole body of typographical devices used to identify and accent elements within the main text, as when you run a list of comments that you want to set off, each indented and preceded by the heavy dot called a *bullet*; or when you box or otherwise set off a quote or extract.

cast off: To cast off is to make an estimate of the number of printed pages that will result from your manuscript, taking different sets of composition assumptions. It is essentially designer's or printer's work, rather than something the self-publisher should attempt to do. If you do decide to try to make the estimate yourself, or are dealing with inexperienced people on the production side, then by all means set a few pages in the type size and style you have selected before making any final decision; then quite literally count the words on the pages set, probably with a computer word-processing program that includes a word-counting feature—or by hand, if necessary. That will give you the average number of words per page, to divide into the total number of words in your manuscript, again probably computer-counted. Then add an estimate for front and back matter to derive the total number of pages. Don't forget to count the sample manuscript pages in your final estimate. Bear in mind that a difference of a single "point" in type-size specifications can make a large difference in the number of pages in your finished book, as can the margins you use. Even two types of the same size may result in books of different size, as one type may be bulkier than the other, and therefore set fewer words on the same size line.

It is also wise to extend this kind of very specific thinking to your choice of book paper. During the process of paper selection, be sure to make up several "dummies," composed of the number of sheets of paper that will result from your estimated number of pages, and using papers of different weights and bulks. Only in that way can you be reasonably sure of the eventual bulk, weight, and therefore "feel" of your book, given the paper chosen. Add a cover sample, and weigh the resulting blank book, with packing materials. You will also then know approximately how much it will cost you to mail the book later on.

character, character count: A character is a single letter or space. It has become an increasingly important device as computer technology has moved into publishing and printing, as more and more cost estimates are stated in characters, rather than words or pages. For example, you may be quoted a composition price of $2.75 per thousand characters, and will need to relate that price to your manuscript. To do so, you will need to make an estimate of the number of characters on the printed page of the book you are doing, given your type and format choices. A preliminary move can be to show the "per character" compositor sample pages, drawn from other books, and ask how much each page would cost to set; only in these ways will you get proper comparison shopping composition estimates.

computer composition: Any way of setting type that uses a computer to perform the main typesetting function is properly described as computer composition. This includes everything from production of a floppy disk using a word-processing program on a smallish home computer to the use of sophisticated—and very expensive—computers that can receive data from remote locations and use it to directly drive high-speed composing machines as part of unified composition-to-printed-page systems that can go from first-draft writing to finished publications.

co-op ad, advertising allowance: Publishers often share the cost of advertising with chain and independent booksellers. When such cost-sharing is done with specific ad placements, the resulting ads are called *co-op* (for *cooperative*) *ads*. When publisher cost-sharing is more general, as when it is expressed as a percentage of a bookseller's cost up to a fixed limit, or as a percentage of a bookseller's purchases from the publisher, the resulting arrangement is an *advertising allowance*. Small self-publishers should seriously consider such cost-sharing arrangements, especially locally and regionally, within budget considerations, as the bookseller who will spend some money to advertise your book is likely to place it well and sell it aggressively.

copy editor: An editor who works over copy already written and prepares it for publication, both by improving the clarity and correctness of exposition and by specifically instructing the compositor on matters concerning composition, such as style, typeface, and design—in self-publishing always subject to the approval of the author-publisher. A light copy editing may involve little more than a quick check for errors in punctuation, grammar, and consistency, as well as obvious errors, while depth editing (also called developmental editing or line editing) often involves major organizational and rewriting changes.

copyright: This is fully discussed in Chapter 3.

database publishing: Publication of information-based products, such as print, online, and videodisk texts, from the information stored in a database, whether computerized or not. In the major modern sense, any publications generated from bodies of information stored in a computer memory.

desktop publishing: The publishing of computer-designed publications, usually on a small scale and by individuals or small publishers, often online and not print-on-paper at all, though at least equally often in the forms of newsletters, books, and pamphlets. The term was in earlier years used to describe computerized publication design assisted by special desktop publishing software, designed to supplant many traditional publication design forms and costs, but has come to be much more widely used to describe any kind of computer-assisted publishing, with or without special software.

dirty copy, penalty copy: These are discussed fully in Chapter 5.

discount: Not so long ago, publishers offered two basic kinds of discounts to their customers. The *long discount* was 40 percent off the list price, the price on the cover of the book; the *short discount* was 20 percent off the list price. The long discount was offered on books offered primarily to booksellers for resale to consumers; the short discount was offered on books sold primarily to libraries and other institutions. For some rather complex reasons having to do with antitrust law, you could not—and still cannot—offer both discounts at the same time, which means that a decision to go with a short, 20 percent, discount effectively guarantees that your book will not be routinely stocked by booksellers, who feel they cannot make enough profit to justify stocking it at that discount. Therefore, the only books likely to be sold at the 20 percent discount are large and expensive reference books unlikely to be bought by most consumers.

In recent years, with jobbers and chains increasingly influencing the bookselling scene, life has become somewhat more complicated for author-publishers—and more difficult. Books headed for libraries are still arranged much as they were, with library jobbers taking more than they used to, but not greatly affecting the publisher's margins from library sales. But bookseller sales are far less lucrative per unit, as chains are routinely demanding and getting 50–52 percent discounts, and jobbers are doing the same. Self-publishers also using distributors have to figure in distributor's discounts as well, but this has been true all along. Returns of unsold books have also greatly increased in recent years; the double shock of increased discounts and increased returns has made trade book publishing more difficult for author-publishers, and for that matter for all small publishers.

first edition, limited edition: All the books run using the original plates of the work comprise the work's *first edition*, whether run all at once or in several printings. Later, if your book acquires collectible value, all the books in that first edition may be valuable, with the books run in the first printing the most valuable of the lot. For certain special works, you may also do a *limited edition*, which is usually a signed and numbered first printing, with limitation of the size of that printing aimed to increase the value of each of the volumes.

flush left, ragged right, justified, unjustified, proportionally spaced: These terms all refer to the handling of type margins on a page. Other than some poetry, almost all type is set *flush left,* that is with an even left margin for all the lines in the text of a page. Most books are set flush left and with *justified* type, creating the even left and right margins we normally associate with books and other printed materials. *Unjustified* lines are set *ragged right;* that means the margins on the right side of the page are uneven, as in most typescript.

formats: These are fully discussed in Chapter 5.

front matter, preliminary matter, main text, back matter, end matter: These terms are fully discussed in Chapter 3 in the section subtitled "The Elements of the Book." Note that *front matter* and *preliminary matter* are synonyms, as are *back matter* and *end matter.* Also note that no particular order applies to the elements in all books, except that title, copyright, dedication, contents, foreword, preface, and introduction belong at the start, as front matter; while footnotes, which refer to text, must follow text, either in the main text or in back matter or at the end of chapters. As for the rest of the elements, placement in the work is a matter of choice. For example, the index, which usually appears at the back of the book, may, for some large reference books, be placed much more usefully at the beginning of the book. The wide ranges of textual materials, maps, tables, and illustrations generally described as appendices may work best placed variously throughout the book, rather than in the back matter.

ghostwriter, coauthor, developmental editor: A writer who works with you by actually writing all or most of your book for you, while you receive sole credit for writing the book, is called a *ghostwriter*. Such a writer, receiving credit, becomes a *coauthor*. An editor who works with you to write, shape, and rewrite your manuscript is neither, but rather is a *developmental editor*. In practice, there are times when the line between ghostwriter and developmental editor becomes rather fine. (For more on these, see Chapter 4.)

graphics, art, illustrations: In practice, these terms are sometimes used quite interchangeably, although they have rather different meanings. *Graphics* describes all the non-word elements of the book—jacket, cover, page design and other format elements, original art, reproduced art, tables, charts, graphs, and whatever else is not straightforward text. *Art* refers to specific pieces of work, such as illustrations and cover designs, ready to be made up with the text into camera-ready copy and then into plates for printing. *Illustrations* are visual material, such as line cuts, halftones, and color photos, that are placed into the book.

galleys: These are long pages of composed type, set in a single column, which will later be put together with any other desired images, such as illustrations, and made up into pages. A galley proof is a copy of the composed galley on which the author and other readers make changes and corrections. Galleys are now rare, since with computer composition, authors generally get paginated proofs to read. Sometimes these are straight text, without some design elements in place, and so may be called *rough pages*. In years past, some sets of uncorrected galleys were bound and sent out as prepublication copies; even today, bound page proofs are often still referred to as *bound galleys*.

hardcover, hardbound, casebound, paperback, softcover, trade paperback, quality paperback, mass market paperback, looseleaf, comb, press: These can be some fairly confusing synonyms for overlapping publishing forms. *Hardcover, hardbound,* and *casebound* are all synonyms, describing hardcover books of all kinds, whatever their sizes or bindings, as long as contents are sewn or glued into bindings. *Paperback* and *softcover* are synonyms, describing books bound into any kind of soft cover, even if that cover is made of very durable, flexible leather or plastic. *Trade paperback* and *quality paperback* are synonyms, describing higher-priced and usually somewhat larger softcover books than are *mass market paperbacks*. The distinctions between trade and mass market paperbacks have been blurring over the years, however—the main distinction now being between the outlets through which they are marketed. *Looseleaf, comb,* and *press* are kinds of binders in which book contents are held by pressure or in drilled sets, rather than glued in.

heads, subheads, running heads: Heads are any legends topping sections of a work, such as chapter headings or chapter subsections. Some headings are subordinate to other headings; for example, when a chapter is broken up into sections and subsections, all but the chapter heading are called *subheads* and may be arranged in a hierarchy of subheads and sub-subheads. *Running heads* do not relate in the same way; they are the lines of copy on the top (occasionally the bottom) of each page, identifying chapter titles and sometimes book titles or page or section contents. Occasionally they run at the bottom of the page, then being called *running feet*.

image area: The *image area* (also called the *live area* or *live space*) is that portion of a page on which printing of any kind will appear, including any white space contained in that area. Usually it is all that space between the top of the running head at the top of the page and the last printed line of any kind on the page whether text or page numbers, and between the furthest left and right printed lines or characters on the page. Where there are marginal notes or comments, they are part of the image area. Where illustrations *bleed*—that is, go to the trimmed edges of pages—the image area of these pages goes to the ends of the illustrations. Note that often a seemingly small adjustment of margins can result in a considerably smaller or larger image area per page; this is one of the two main means of adjusting the number of pages in the finished book, the other being choice of type size.

in press, on press: In press means that a book is past manuscript and into the production process. *On press* is far more specific, meaning that your book is actually on a press and being run. Self-publishing press runs are usually rather modest, and a book that is on press is quite likely to be run in full once put on press, and then put through bindery and sent out to you rather quickly after that. But a book described to you as being "in press" may very well be stalled somewhere and in need of a push.

libel, slander, invasion of privacy: These are fully discussed in Chapter 3.

line cut, halftone, color separation: These are the three main kinds of illustration reproduction methods used in books, in order of expense. The line cut, a synonym for *line engraving,* is an engraving on a plate, or a reproduction of an engraving, which is then photographically reproduced, as composed text copy is reproduced. This often works quite well visually on the kind of book paper used for text. A *halftone* is a reproduction of a photograph or other image, which must be done through a special screen and results in a dot pattern which can be used to reproduce the original: it usually works better on glossy stock than on normal book paper. *Color separation* refers to the development of a set of printing plates—with primary colors from the original separated out—that when used together during printing can reproduce the color of the original image. Some aspects of the color separation and reproduction techniques are now being superseded by new technology. Color reproductions require glossy stock to work well and are also more expensive to do. If you intend to use some in your book, be keenly aware of their probable high cost and get firm estimates based on samples of the kinds of illustrations you will use before deciding to go ahead.

makeready: This is the process of putting a piece of work on a printing press and preparing it to be run. *Makeready time*—the time it takes to do this—is a very important element of cost for self-publishers, many of whom do short press runs, in which makeready time is a large part of total press time and therefore of book manufacturing cost.

When comparison shopping costs, bear in mind that one press will suit your needs far better than another and that the printers you are talking with will quite naturally try to sell you their services, even though their equipment may not really be right for the job. For example, a wonderfully fast press that is fine for long runs may not be at all good for short runs, because it requires so much time to make ready for printing. Note that those printers who make short runs a substantial part of their business are most likely to have equipment that suits self-publishers' needs.

out of print, out of stock, back ordered: When you have gone temporarily *out of stock* on your book, you plan to reprint. In that situation, orders coming in are *back ordered,* to be fulfilled when you have books again. This is quite different from *out of print,* which in the book trade means that the publisher does not currently plan to reprint the book. Orders placed for an out-of-print book will be canceled, and booksellers will inform retail customers that the book is no longer available. If you are temporarily unable to fill orders but are planning to reprint, be sure you inform those who order that you are out of stock rather than out of print.

perfect bound: Perfect binding, which is a very far from perfect way of binding books, is discussed fully in Chapter 5.

permissions: These are fully discussed in Chapter 3.

presses: There are several good ways of getting ink on paper, and most printers are justifiably proud of their equipment, which has roughly the same place in their scheme of things as your books have in yours. One printer may have a wonderful *web-fed rotary press,* meaning a press that spins around as it prints, fed by a continuous roll of paper, and works very fast—though it may take a comparatively long time to set up. Another may have a *rotary press* that is sheet-fed (that is, fed by a pile of sheets) and works somewhat slower, but takes less time to set up. Another may have a *sheet-fed, flat-bed press,* the other main job shop press in use today, which is just right for you in makeready time and speed, but of not quite the right size for your book, so that you waste a lot of paper in printing. Another may be enormously proud of having acquired a *jet press*, which—like most high-speed computer printers—sprays ink on paper as it goes by, works tremendously fast, and may be wholly inappropriate for your publishing needs because of its high setup costs. Your concern as a publisher is to get the most efficient organization and presses you can find working to produce your books cost effectively. You are unlikely to go far wrong if you limit your inquiries and comparison shopping to experienced short-run book printers.

prepublication: This is fully discussed in Chapter 5.

proofs: Several kinds of proofs are fully discussed in Chapter 5.

rights: Several kinds of rights are fully discussed in Chapter 6.

saddle-stitching, Smythe sewing, side-stitching: These and other binding methods are fully discussed in Chapter 5.

selection, main selection, alternate selection, coselection, dividend: A *selection* is a book club purchase of multiple copies of your book or the right to print their own edition of your book. A *main selection* is that book the club will send its members without their asking for it, unless their members exercise their right to turn down the book within a specified period (which is called the exercise of a *negative option*). An *alternate selection* is a book that members may choose instead of, or as well as, the main selection. A *coselection* means that your book is teamed up with another book, the two sold together to members as a single selection. A *dividend* is the use of your book as an inducement or premium, as when copies can be purchased by prospective members for one dollar when they join the book club, or when it is supplied free or at very low cost to all those current members who have purchased a certain number of books.

serif, sans serif. Beware the book designer or compositor who suggests that you set your book in a lovely, modern sans serif type. *Serifs* are small projections off the ends of letters, added to give more body to the typeface; most classic and widely used bookfaces have them. Typefaces characterized by the presence of serifs also vary the thicknesses of the body of the type. *Sans serif* means without a serif; typefaces without serifs also tend to have no variation in body thicknesses, instead having letters of uniform thickness. Sans serif typefaces are widely used for some kinds of periodicals and in advertising; they are much less successful as book typefaces, as most tend to develop pages that are monotonous and therefore hard to read.

signatures: These are fully discussed in Chapter 5.

trade book: A *trade book* is a book that is sold through trade outlets, which are bookstores and other outlets selling directly to consumers. Such a book may also be sold by mail and to libraries and other institutions. The identification as a trade book stems more from the kind of discount offered (generally 40 percent or higher) and the selling price than from the content of the book. Nor are the distinctions between the kinds of books terribly clear. A book of reference selling at $40 but carrying a 40 percent discount will be described by some people in the publishing and bookselling trades as a reference book and by others as a trade book. If you wish to try to sell your book through trade outlets, offer the trade discount, accept returns for full credit, and describe your book as a trade book, whatever its content and however else you sell it.

type sizes, point system: These are discussed fully in Chapter 5.

vanity publishing: This is fully discussed in Chapter 1.

INDEX

....